BACH, THE MASTER

A NEW INTERPRETATION OF HIS GENIUS

BACH

BACH, THE MASTER

A New Interpretation of
His Genius

By

RUTLAND BOUGHTON

HARPER & BROTHERS
New York and London
1930

3622

To
CIRCE
in grateful revenge

CONTENTS

ILLUSTRATIONS

FOREWORD

FORKEL and Spitta secured the knowledge of Bach and his work. Dr. Albert Schweitzer has since given convincing suggestions for the interpretation of that work. Parry and others have written enlightening studies. Professor Sanford Terry has made laborious and invaluable investigations, and has recently published a Life which enables us to realize much more vividly than before the external conditions which influenced the master.

Is it impertinent to believe that it still remains to show something of the relation between the man and his work?—for it seems to me that Bach's compositions were not the objective things they are generally believed to be—and not only to show something of the relation between the man and his work, but something also of the relation between that work and the civilization of which Bach's art is perhaps the finest flower.

Properly to study an art which took a lifetime to achieve would itself be the work of a lifetime. I cannot pretend that I have done more than give a few hints along the line chosen.

The more fully to make this book useful to students I have refrained from using music-type examples, and referred them, whenever possible, to such gramophone records as I have been able to discover. By this means I hope that they will be the better able to relate the general argument of the book to the living sound of the master's art.

My indebtedness has to be expressed to Mr. David Scott and Messrs. Novello and Company for the loan of music; to Mr. Arthur Brooks, artistic director of the Columbia Gramophone Company, and to the Educational Department of The Gramophone Company (H.M.V.) for help in the choice of illustrations; to the magistracy of Lüneberg for information regarding St. Michael's Convent; to others for permission to quote from their English translations. So far as possible I have used as the basis of my argument works of which such translations are available.

R. B.

BACH, THE MASTER

Chapter One

THE GREATEST COMPOSER

THERE was in the life of John Sebastian Bach a tragedy which has never been explored, nor even touched with any degree of imaginative consideration. Spitta seems to have been puzzled by it. Schweitzer alludes to it almost in a tone of annoyance. Doctor Sanford Terry in his recent *Life* refers to it sympathetically, but does not follow up its significance in the composer's creative career. The tragedy is that of an artist whose inmost nature and external material conditions are in irreconcilable opposition— who is forced by circumstances to devote his life to a kind of spiritual service in which he has no faith, and is necessarily false either to that service or to himself.

Such an opposition in the lives of ordinary men does not matter very much. It seems of comparatively little account that a royalist general should become president of a republic, or a socialist journalist serve upon a conservative newspaper; but the power of a creative artist is exerted in his capacity for emotional revelation: if an artist's emotions are violated his life-work is bound to be thwarted. A man may be false to

~1~

his intellect, and retain his self-respect by a latitudinarian or cynical attitude to life; but no man may be false to his feeling and maintain his creative integrity. A man may say a thing which he does not believe—sign a state document or newspaper article which expresses thoughts in regard to which he is indifferent or even opposed, earn a living by so doing and perhaps never be found out, or, if found out, tolerated and even admired for his 'breadth of view'; but a creative artist dare not so endanger his inmost veracity. Once an artist is false to his feelings his imaginative power is definitely weakened; and if he pursues the falsehood his power finally deserts him.

Artists of noble conservative mind—Sophocles, Chaucer, Spenser, Shakespeare, Angelico, Haydn, and Mendelssohn, to name a few—seem to have found no essential opposition between their own natures and the mental atmosphere in which their lives were passed; but others, and perhaps a majority of the greatest, have been less fortunate. Some have been broken like Botticelli and Mozart. Some have saved their integrity by frank rebellion like Dante, Beethoven and Shelley. Others, like Goya and Blake, have preserved their principles by wrapping them up in obscure form; or by the use of allegory and symbolism, like Michel Angelo and Rabelais. Others again, like Wagner, Wordsworth, and Bernard Shaw, have striven for a time, but finally taken up a more generally acceptable attitude, an attitude which has been inconsistent with their most typical and virile work.

The thread of these chapters will be strung with instances of the method which Bach used to maintain his essential individuality and faith in a world to which he was opposed. I am not referring to such difficulties as artists frequently have in the management of their business affairs. That is generally a comedy rather than a tragedy. I am referring to the need which Bach had to give expression to feelings which were in direct opposition to the pretences and declarations of the world wherein only he could get a livelihood.

Even Bach's tragedy was not without its comic aspects. When he and his fellow musicians first performed the music which is now generally believed to be the greatest the world has known, they were dressed as to their bodies in garments which were not uncomely; but they were crowned with monstrosities in the way of head-gear. A picture exists of musicians playing in St. Thomas's Church at Leipsig a few years before Bach's appointment as Cantor; and it is hard to associate the complete artificiality of the scene with the nature of the music they were presently to usher into being. But it was not only the musicians who were hidden under masses of false hair. Long before he got to Leipsig Bach had found it necessary to put a wig upon his art;

and for a long time the wig has obscured a proper understanding of that art.

To the generation immediately succeeding his own Bach seemed all wig. For the people of that time he was merely a great organist and fugal theorist. His art was almost forgotten. Later on his music was rediscovered, but because a new conception of music had arisen —a new fashion in wigs—the formal side of Bach's art loomed larger than it did even in his own time. He was therefore accounted a great master of 'ideal' music, which, being translated into human terms, means music which has no clear relation to reality. In that æsthetic faith Spitta wrote the monumental *Life* which has weighed down upon the real Bach like the most expensive kind of cemetery memorial. The thousand and one details which showed that the music had a very intimate relation to the material world, and above all its realistic themes, were regarded as little clouds in a great blue sky.

Then Dr. Albert Schweitzer published his remarkable study, drawing special attention to those very details—showing that, far from clouding the broad heaven of Bach's music, they were, on the contrary, stars and constellations throwing their light upon its dark and mysterious places—showing how they increased the general significance of the art in a manner comparable with the realistic details of Gothic sculpture, or the leading themes in the music-dramas of Wagner.

MUSICIANS PLAYING IN ST. THOMAS'S CHURCH AT LEIPSIG

The effect of Schweitzer's work was as if he had taken the wig off old Bach's head and shown us the living man at work in his study.

Considering all that has been elaborated by wiser and more knowledgable men than I, it will probably seem arrogant if I say that it still remains to show Bach as man and artist in relation to European culture; but one mistake which has arisen as a result of the wider interest in his music, is the idea that his art now really belongs to us. The greatest master of music has become a popular name in concert-programmes, and there is a danger that his essential greatness may be smothered by our æsthetic love and wonder.

Musicians disagree in most matters concerning music; but regarding the supreme greatness of Bach they are unanimous. Pedants and idealists, antiquarians and realists, futurists and quite ordinary musicians find common ground there. The enjoyment of the music, and a certain limited understanding of it, have extended beyond the sphere of cultured musicians to the widest circles of the amateur world.

Bach packs the houses for cheap promenade concerts. Festivals devoted exclusively to Bach's music have been given in several of our chief cities, and choirs specially formed to study his works; while no musical festival is counted adequate unless its programme includes at least one of his major compositions. Scanning the concert-posters in a music-shop the other day I noticed that four of nine related to programmes of Bach's music.

When a man's work is being studied to such an extent there seems the less need to talk and write about it, especially as one of the chief faults of Anglo-Saxon cultural life is an excess of books and lectures and a general lack of active artistic recreation. So it would be foolish if the growing practice of Bach's music should be diverted to a paper appreciation of it, to say nothing of the fact that the sheer greatness of the subject might well cause a better man than I to falter before the job.

But one thing outweighs my diffidence and laziness— it is a growing sense that this appreciation of the greatest of all music is a temporary and partly a pathological thing, and less to our credit than we may like to think.

A longing for beautiful sights and sounds will certainly accompany any rising civilization; but that longing is by no means stilled during periods of decadence, and has in fact been very much in evidence during periods when the creative faculty has seemed weak and exhausted. Our enjoyment of Bach's music may possibly arise from an understanding of, and sympathy with, the forces which combined to make it great; but our enjoyment may, on the other hand, arise from our own incapacity and cowardice as men of the world, who, having no power to make enduring musical beauty of our own, are obliged to fall back on the greatest that

was made at a time when a genius and a generation remembered what it was to live greatly.

Up to the year 1914 the stream of contemporary
European music ran emotionally and even sentimen-
tally. Before the war the outstanding living composer
was Richard Strauss. His music moved from the most
trivial and sentimental planes of 'Love in the Gloam-
ing' and 'The Baby in the Bath' to the most grandiose
and lurid expressions of the 'Self as Hero' and the
'Sadist as Heroine.' Some of us who had enjoyed that
music before the war had a curious and shamefast sense
of disillusionment when we heard it again afterwards.
Could this flaring tawdriness, this pretentious romanticism, this petty love-slushing, be the same music which
five years earlier had seemed to rank its maker with
the great masters of music?

Of course, it was we ourselves who had changed. The
reality, the exhausting reality of the war, had devital-
ised us, and we needed emotional rest. That, I think,
accounts not only for the exposure of what was weak
in Strauss, but also for the revival of primitive music
and of primitivism in modern music. If this diagnosis
is correct it will account also for the extraordinary
post-war popularity of Bach's music, in which is concentrated and enlarged all the values of those composers who had preceded him, and even the values
of some who followed him. Byrd, Palestrina, Couperin, and Schütz—Monteverde and Gesualdo—Mo-

zart and Brahms—having nothing of great musical adventure which is not already implicit, and generally explicit, in the music of John Sebastian.

For British people the oratorios of Handel had hitherto served the highest general need; and the pre-war popularity of Handel was, of course, something more than a purely musical appreciation. It had to some extent become a habit, but was still more vital than a mere vogue, as were the passing popularities of Gounod and Tschaikovsky, and even of Sullivan.

This is not the place to discuss Handel's greatness; but to understand the good and the bad in the tendency of to-day, when the art of Handel is obviously being superseded by the art of Bach, we must briefly consider the function served by the lesser master's oratorios in the story of 'unmusical England.'

Handel's first attempts in England, and his first successes, were in the opera-house. Opera was then, as now, the toy of the wealthy classes rather than the joy of the masses. Occasional enthusiasts excepted, the wealthy have never been noted in any country or period for their constancy in the appreciation of the arts. Art has been for them a means of killing time rather than of making it more alive. They pass from one art-vogue to another as from one dress fashion to another. So Handel inevitably came to grief. Luckily he was stranded upon the bank where he discovered the oratorio, a form of art exactly suiting the suppressed emotions of the respectable British middle classes at that time, and for a considerable time afterwards.

Ecclesiastical authority having put a ban upon Handel's opera on the subject of Esther—the objection being to the sacredness of the matter!—the composer discovered that the ordinary run of people preferred the lesser degree of emotional stimulus which results when dramatic situations are discussed, rather than the fuller experience which accompanies a presentation of the same situations in the theatre.

A few centuries earlier it had been one of the chief joys of the common people to give dramatic representations of sacred subjects: they were then the chief material for drama, and were not merely encouraged, but actually performed by officials of the church. The gradual suppression of the Christian mystery plays from the time of the Reformation was accompanied throughout Europe by the more or less forced cultivation of a bastard Hellenism; and it is not without significance for our understanding of the tragedy in Bach's mental life that the thing in process of suppression had a communist ethic, while the thing which supplanted it had an opposite tendency, the original human values of the Greek stories having been subverted by Roman decadents and imperialists.

Handel was approved for a time in English governing circles. The approval coincided with his Græco-Roman period. His embarrassing reversion to stories from the Bible—however harmless the stories and similar to the Greek in the fact of their legendary origin—was a definite flouting of the prevailing dogma that art ought to be meaningless and exist merely for beauty's sake, or for the sake of those who had time to kill, money to spend, and demanded amoral amusement.

William Blake came up against the same difficulty a few years later, and was filled with a sort of divine fury against those who 'set up the stolen and perverted writings of Homer and Ovid, Plato and Cicero, against the sublime of the Bible.'

The fact was that in the popular view the Jewish scriptures and Christian gospels were still the chief measure of human life and conduct. It was impossible for the public mind to regard anything taken from the Bible as other than a direct encouragement or rebuke in matters of belief and behaviour. It was equally a part of the mind of the governing classes to regard Christian ethic as subversive of business morality, while even the broader ideas of the Old Testament were sometimes inconvenient.

Having appealed from the court to the people, and even to the people of the provinces—from the lesser public to the greater—Handel met with his reward. It was not the variable and passing reward of popular success, though that was in some measure his also; it was the permanent reward which follows when a real addition is made to the records of life and imagination.

In the oratorios of Handel the public (though comparatively lacking in fineness of spirit owing to the inhuman foundations of their increasing wealth) found not merely a healthy amusement, but an expression of the best part of their religious belief. For them Handel's art was not merely a thing of beauty; it was also a divine service and an act of faith.

Those oratorios remained the chief expression of noble emotion in England until 1914. They took a major place at the great festivals in spite of the growing Bach-worship among professional musicians, and in spite of the steady increase of power among native composers from Sullivan to Elgar.

However, the war broke down not only the regular musical activities of Britain, but our last Christian pretensions as well. Before the war Handel's place was maintained in our programmes by the insistence of the musical laity, and in the face of professional boredom and critical derision. After the war, with its violation of all that Christians had professed to believe, there was no vital religious opinion remaining. The churches stood like lamps whose last feeble flames had flickered out.

The religious function of Handel's music having ceased, it was inevitable, on artistic grounds that his greater contemporary should take his place.

Bach came to his kingdom, not as a great religious artist, but as the greatest of all musical composers—a

composer so great that he was never obliged to emphasize, and rarely even draw attention to, his emotional
background; a composer of such intellectual and architectural skill that he was acceptable even to the younger
men, who were fed up with feeling too much.

When emotionalism was scorned, and rightly scorned,
in the bored annoyance of the young musicians, the
vital importance of emotion itself was prejudiced. It
is none the less certain that without a core of emotion
there can be no music, no living art of any kind. Therefore when we harked back to the music of earlier times,
seeking in its incapacity for full expressiveness a means
of mental quiet and healing, we were to some extent
forswearing the real world. Indeed the genuine development of musical faculty to-day has not yet reached
any degree of real creativeness just because it is to some
extent a mental retirement, instead of the expression of
our will to face the world, and make it better than it
now is.

In so far as the present love of Bach's music is caused
by a dissatisfaction with real life—in so far as it represents a wish, conscious or unconscious, to discover an
inner world which shall be less disappointing than the
outer world which promised homes for heroes and
grudges them their bread, which proposed a League of
Nations to end war and proceeds to use the League
with a view to a war on a larger scale than before—
in so far as our love for this greatest of all music is

connected with our disappointment and fear, it is an evil sign, lulling us to inaction instead of serving as an emotional tonic.

The tonic possibilities of Bach's music are great. No other music can approach it in that respect. To use this music when we are really seeking a sedative is the final irony in the tragedy of Bach. But the rightful values of his art will only appear if we understand how it came about. So I write these pages as a musician for wiser students of life, as a student of life for better musicians, in the hope of showing something of Bach's creative position in the story of Christian civilization, rather than with a will once more to trace the story of his external life, or offer another æsthetic outline of his art. This will, I hope, be read by musicians who are more penetrating than I in matters of æsthetic, by lovers of men and women who are more penetrating than I in matters of psychology. If a few of them find validity enough in the general argument to make my mistakes worth correcting, and the argument itself worth pursuing into matters of art and happiness beyond my understanding and competency, the labour will have been well spent.

But first a consideration of the understanding which Bach's music has already reached in the minds of music-lovers.

When it was first resurrected by Zelter, Mendelssohn, and others, among those who enthusiastically responded were Goethe and Hegel. However, though the music was admired, the words it enshrined were generally disapproved. Zelter objected not only to the nature of the librettos, but to what he called 'French froth' in the music. That froth he proposed to skim off, though he seems to have ignored Goethe's enquiry as to how the skimming was to be done.

When Mendelssohn revived the St. Matthew Passion he cut a good deal of it, including many arias; and, as we shall see later on, it is in the arias that Bach enshrined a vital part of his Christian realism.

When Peters, the music publisher, proposed to issue *Bach's Complete Works*, it was generally understood that only instrumental music was intended!

For music lovers of that time Bach was a 'musical poet' (Forkel) attaining 'great expression by the profound development and inexhaustible combination of simple ideas' (Rochlitz). The creative power was admitted right enough, but no attempt was made to look for its cause. The words of the vocal works would have given many a clue to that cause; but the words were regarded as the foolish expression of religious principles and fashions of a previous and fanatic generation. What remained of value in the music was apparently a great rocky grandeur barnacled with childish realisms, and foamy with French froth.

Here and there a creative mind would press more deeply into the music, and find signs of a religion which had either been half-conceived or was already half-scorned, half-forgotten. Thus Schumann wrote to Mendelssohn, "You confessed to me that if life were to deprive you of hope and faith, this one chorale [1] would bring it back again to you.

Spitta's great biography was the climax of the appreciation of Bach as an orthodox musician. It was written with the idea of exalting the master; in effect it diminished him. The biographer's final summary was that Bach's works were 'the highest outcome of an essentially national art whose origin lies in the period of the Reformation.'

The fact is that the ears of Spitta, and of most musicians of his generation, were closed to the significance of those realistic suggestions which illumine Bach's vocal works more vividly than ever colour-artist illuminated the words of a missal. The biographer knew that the suggestions were there: those hints of material things like swords and spears, seas and rivers, serpents and asses, whips and wings; but for the 'pure musicians' of the time such things were abominations, excrescences needing elaborate explanation, condonation, and apology.

Having got rid of those clues to the real nature of Bach's art, Spitta was obliged to account for the greatness of his subject in terms of mystical rhetoric. [2] Then

[1] The chorale-prelude, "O schmücke dich, O liebe Seele."
[2] See for example the end of Chapter 3 in Book IV, of the biography.

he claps a half-shorn wig back on the head of the god he has set up in his own image, and the general puzzlement is complete. Bach becomes a 'classical' composer, bugbear of children's piano lessons, and most intimate crony of musical pedants and highbrows.

Less narrow and unreal conceptions of Bach's art had been proposed even in the earliest days of his posthumous appreciation. Hegel said that it had passed 'from the merely melodic to the characteristic,' though he qualified the value of his appreciation by adding that 'the melodic remains justified as the sustaining and uniting soul.' Still, the recognition that with Bach music passed from its archaic and scientific stage to a vehicle for the apt expression of human character was a great step in understanding.

A more simple, but in some ways more adequate, idea of the music was stated in 1845 by Mosewius, a musician of Breslau. 'Bach represents standing and moving, resting and hurrying, with a naïveté almost characteristic of the first beginnings of art. Without abandoning this minute detail-painting in later works, his method now becomes as it were transfigured. His thought, vision, and emotion have remained unchanged, but in the later works the tone-painting is not so isolated.' [1]

No proper understanding, however, of the nature

[1] Quoted by Schweitzer, I, 247 of English translation by Ernest Newman.

of Bach's art was possible until after the publication of Schweitzer's great study. That showed how the manifold realistic details of the music were signs of a vitality which is absent from 'pure art,' and offered a general key to the master's tone-language. We are now able to recognize the relation between the art of Bach and, for example, the art of Dürer, and even, as Mosewius glimpsed, the figure-sculpture of the best Gothic.

When such realistic detail is prominent in the music Schweitzer generally refers to it as 'dramatic.' He very truly says that in a certain sense it was Wagner who made Bach intelligible. It is quite true that until modern musicians had become accustomed to Wagner's habit of leading motives they were very much confused in their appreciation of Bach's realisms. But a use of realistic details does not make a drama unless they are combined in dramatic relation. It was the apparent absence of such dramatic scheme which threw Spitta and his like back on the mere music 'as the sustaining and uniting soul.' They were at any rate justified in demanding something more from a composer than a childish love of imitation; and Bach's realisms would indeed be childish games and crudities unless by their means his art were placed in a more comprehensive relation to the general culture.

In this particular matter Schweitzer does not take us very much further than Spitta did, though without Schweitzer's imaginative revelation any complete understanding would still be impossible. The word 'dramatic' has thus far been vaguely, and sometimes incorrectly, applied to the art of Bach; and we may be helped to an even more complete enjoyment of his works if we can discover why the master was obliged to take a dramatic rather than a purely lyrical attitude for works which (excepting only the Passions) convey little of drama as the word is understood to-day.

Bach often expressed the thoughts and feelings of others in a dramatic way, but he was generally expressing his own as well; and, still more vital to the purpose of the present study, he was continuing a traditional expression of immense power and importance —an expression with which his own personality was generally identified, in which his own ideas had their validity. That tradition, having its source in the greatest period of Christian civilization, was recognized by Spitta so far as the art of music was concerned, and by Schweitzer in that he associates Bach with medieval rather than with Renaissance art. And there, so far, the understanding seems to end. It is even possible for Schweitzer to say, 'In the case of no other artist has the external course of his life so little to do with the origin of his works,'[1] a statement which I think will seem mistaken before we have gone very far.

Schweitzer's sense that Bach's was a dramatic genius is right enough; but not once in the course of his other-

[1] Schweitzer, I, 256.

wise splendid study does he indicate what the drama was
which Bach was making or enacting. The play, the grim
drama was there right enough. It was nothing less than
the crucifixion of Christendom. In the effort to give
expression to that drama in the teeth of a world that
was gross, stupid, cruel, and hypocritical, Bach fulfilled
the tragedy of his career.

⚬⚬ Chapter Two ⚬⚬

THE DECLINE OF CHRISTENDOM

A<small>T THE</small> beginning of the eighteenth century a German musician had the choice of three courses of life. He could take domestic service with a member of the ruling class; he could serve an ecclesiastical body—in North Germany the semi-public service of Protestant organizations, in South Germany the more aristocratic service of the Roman Church; or he could enjoy the freedom and uncertainties of vagrancy.

Bach's career was spent partly in the menial service of petty princes, partly in the more respectable position of a public official. To understand properly the incidents of his life and the nervous obstinacy of his mind, we must try to get an idea of the general atmosphere in which he lived.

The communal Christianity of the Middle Ages reached its climax somewhere between the years 1200 and 1300. The chief evidence of that climax is, of course, the building of the Gothic cathedrals under conditions of such general participation and popular joy as seems to us almost incredible.

Notre Dame was finished and Rouen begun in 1208. Rheims was commenced in 1211. Amiens and Salisbury and the west front of Peterborough date from 1220. Beauvais was begun in 1225, York in 1230, the choir of Rheims completed in 1241, while the Bamberg figure-sculpture which Professor Flinders Petrie looks upon as the peak of Christian masonry, belongs to 1245. Lincoln was finished in 1255, Amiens in 1257 and Salisbury the following year, while in 1260 was consecrated that Chartres for which 'nobles, merchants, craftsmen and peasants gave—some money, some provisions—all gave labour, harnessing themselves to carts to drag the stone. Our Lady worked many miracles at her shrine at Chartres; but the greatest miracle was the human expression that the *work* of building wrought as its gift to the interests of life. . . . This may read to moderns as the dream romance of a William Morris, but it seemed gospel to the times of St. Francis and St. Louis.' [1]

Such amazing activity in forms of art and loveliness seems to have no parallel in the history of the world— the greater part of a continent engaged chiefly in the service of what was really noble and, as Professor Prior emphasizes, dedicated to the service of life—this life here on earth. But perhaps readers are wondering what it all has to do with Bach? Let me remind them that

[1] Professor Prior's *Eight Chapters on Medieval Art*, and Professor Petrie's *The Revolutions of Civilisation*.

Spitta, Schweitzer, and all who have carefully studied
the matter, agree that the art of Bach is the musical
culmination of the same spirit which produced those
cathedrals. Bach belonged, not to the Renaissance culture which was already strong in his own time and has
prevailed since, but to the culture which flowered out
so wonderfully in the Middle Ages as a result of the
common will to establish the Kingdom of Heaven here
on earth.

Let us recall also a fact which, especially since the
war, is apt to be forgotten—the Christian civilization of
the Middle Ages was mainly a German civilization.
Lombard and Frank, Saxon and Fleming belonged to
the same blood stream. The more northerly and east-
erly of the German tribes were later in accepting the
symbols of Christianity, it is true; so that a superficial
or interested interpretation of history has labelled that
civilization a Latin rather than a German thing; but
from the time of Charlemagne to the time of Bach
German influence was evident in all noble Christian
growth; and it was the common people, and especially
the peasantry, of Central Europe who maintained the
most stubborn fight for the communal principles of
Christianity at the close of the Middle Ages; whereas
the Latin, Greek, and Celtic folk were comparatively
easily overcome by the tyranny which accompanied the
changes of thought at the Renaissance.

It is impossible to trace here the complete cultural

line of progress from the sculptural work of the cathedral masons, through the mural paintings of the artisans and the more developed pictures of northern Italy, through the literature which reached its crest in Dante and the Lutheran and English Bibles, until finally the art of Bach became inevitable, and was developed as a direct consequence of all that had gone before; but we must get rid of any idea that those various wonders of the human hand and brain had any sort of national origin.

Internationalism was an essential part of the Christian creed; and if the outstanding examples of human energy and sympathy were concentrated at one time in Eastern France, at another in Florence, and later in England and Saxony, it happened so because mental energy had special freedom and favour in those places at those times. The significance of all the expressions was the same. What Chartres said in stone, Giotto said in pigment, More in literature, and Bach in music. Some of the superficial characteristics of Renaissance art are to be found in that same painting, literature, and music. That was because the climax and downfall of Christian principles in action and politics had been reached before the art of painting had matured, and before literature and music had fairly developed as consciously contrived arts. It is a fact of special importance for our present consideration.

An early indication of Christian decadence was the

authorised attack in 1209 upon the Albigenses, a folk whose lives were so exemplary that they were known as 'the good men.' Unfortunately they offended the ecclesiastical officials because their creed tended to the rationalization of theological dogma, as did the whole tendency of the finest art of the period. When the officials of the Christian Church decided to throw in their lot with the forces of finance and commerce it was necessary to keep the people in subjection by means of their superstitions; but the transformation of mystical phrases into their rational equivalents is a work which must always accompany the ascent of a people from slavery to freedom, unless a religion is to be abandoned with the superstitions of a people's mental immaturity.

Among later signs of the climax was the election in 1271 of Pope Gregory X, "a man who really aimed at the good of Christendom," with whom "the series of great popes ended." But throughout the thirteenth century there were sinister evidences of opposition to the growth of popular freedom and the general welfare. Perhaps the most significant was the connivance of the papacy itself with the practice of usury, although 'the taking of interest on loans was forbidden to Christians.'[1]

Victory went, however, to the clerical officials and their financial masters; and one of the things we have to bear in mind throughout the course of our present

[1] Sismondi, *History of the Italian Republics*; and Thorndike, *Medieval Europe.*

study is the need for showing the essential matters—
the solid and material human considerations—which
lurk behind the religious terminology.

Reaction gathered force, the original and material
struggle having gone against the communal conception
of Christianity; until in Bach's day the strife persisted
only in terms of theology.

Dante's exile in 1302 may be said to mark the definite
defeat of the Christian cause. The terminological strife
continued and increased; but though the peoples of
Europe were divided into Catholic and Protestant, and
cross-torn in national and even parochial units, the
warring leaders, commercial and ecclesiastical, and the
remains of the feudal reactionaries, could always be
relied on to unite against the common people, whose
struggle towards power had synchronised with the most
wonderful achievements of Christian art. Religion, from
being an international and binding force, was subordinated to the cunning ideals of patriotism and national
jealousy; and the energies which were previously fer-
tilised to productions of beauty were now directed to
the interests of commerce, of personal ambition and
greed.

During the fifteenth and sixteenth centuries the
struggle was carried on by the Hussites of Bohemia and
the followers of Münzer in the Bachs' own land of
Thuringia. Though the strife was bloody, and material

interests were the decisive factors, the fight seems to have been expressed almost entirely in terms of theology.

Everywhere the Reformation had a definite economic aspect: the struggle was not, as orthodox historians would have us believe, chiefly a struggle between two divergent views regarding the right way to worship a god. Nor was it entirely a struggle between a decadent feudal system and the earlier forces of capitalistic growth. There was a third party in the field, the common people, whose material interests were bound up with the triumph or failure of the original Christian ethic. Consequently, even when the theological disputants compromised (as they did from time to time to serve their temporary material interests), and even later on when the feudal and capitalistic classes became merged and united against the common folk, the battle was maintained. The obstinate character of the German people, and especially of the peasantry, resulted in a more or less continuous state of popular rebellion, even down to the time of Bach.

At the end of the seventeenth century it was still the peasantry, with the somewhat unreliable help of the free towns (so called) which whole-heartedly continued the struggle against the enemy, whose stronghold was then the court of Louis XIV of France—and that in spite of the 'unscrupulous desertion' of their own German princes.[1] Even so late as the early eighteenth century the common people still led the van of the Christian cause; and it was they who continually paid the penalty of failure.

The reign of terror which they endured from the time of the treachery of Pope Clement V in the fourteenth century to the time of the French Revolution in the eighteenth was inevitable if mercantile and industrial activity were to be carried on in a manner definitely opposed to original Christian doctrine. The terror was a means of forcing the people into new paths of economic slavery; and the functionaries of the churches, Roman and Protestant, could almost always be relied on to support the anti-Christian cause.

No one, perhaps, peasant or prince, merchant or priest, saw it in that way. For the governing class it seemed a fight between common sense and an ideal from fairyland—between the solid facts of the increasing luxury and power the minority were enjoying, and the tiresome and outworn rules of a faith that had failed. For the workers it seemed a simple opposition between those who had more than they needed and themselves who had less than enough. The majority of the people accordingly held fast by Christian tradition: they believed that the Kingdom of God could, and still would, come upon earth, on such terms of human equality as

[1] Menzel, *History of Germany*, English translation (Bohn ed.), III, 498.

were implicit in Christian doctrine; and in their masters they saw men who were definitely in the service of the devil, making an end of human brotherhood for the sake of money and things of corruption.

Thuringia, the homeland of the Bachs, had been a chief centre of the Peasants' War. There the suppressed passion for human freedom had become a no less passionate argument in obscure phrases of theology. For some of the sceptical master-class the theological strife may have seemed a safety valve for pent revolutionary feeling. For the people themselves mystical phraseology was the verbal currency of a vital and baulked desire. A reversion to physical strife was by no means an impossibility. The Thuringians, like the majority of the peoples of Europe, regarded the leading prince of the time as the leading anti-Christian because his methods were anti-popular. The outward adhesion of Louis XIV to the Roman Church damned the church in the eyes of the people instead of sanctifying the king; and all the petty German princes who took their cue from Louis were naturally damned with him, whether their religious profession were Roman or Lutheran.

Menzel, writing from the point of view of the middle classes, says that in 'The Grand Monarch' was accomplished the first revolution against the Middle Ages:

'He said with truth, I am the State! for entire France, the country and the people, were his. The sole object of the entire nation was to do the will of their sovereign. For it is Our Pleasure, was the usual termination to his commands. The magnificent chateau of Versailles, the abode of this terrestrial deity, was peopled with mistresses and a countless troupe of parasites, on whom the gold drawn from the impoverished and oppressed people, was lavished. The nobility and clergy, long subject to their lord and king, shared the licence of the court, and formed a numerous band of courtiers, whilst men of the lower classes, whose superior parts had brought them into note, were attached as philosophers, poets and artists, to the court, the monarch extending his patronage to every art and science prostituted by flattery. The French Court, although externally Catholic, was solely guided by the tenets of the new philosophy, which were spread over the rest of the world by the sonnets of anacreontic poets and the bon-mots of court savants. This philosophy set forth that egotism was the only quality natural to man, that virtues were but feigned, or when real ridiculous. Freedom from the ancient prejudice of religion or honour, and carelessness in the choice of means for the attainment of an object, were regarded as proofs of genius. Immorality was the necessary accompaniment of talent. Virtue implied stupidity; the grossest licence the greatest wit. Vice became the mode, was publicly displayed and admired. The first duty imposed upon knighthood, the protection of innocence, was exchanged for seduction, adultery, or nightly orgies, and the highest ambition of the prince, the courtier, or the officer, was to enrich the *chronique scandaleuse* with his name. A courtier's honour consisted in breaking his word, in deceiving maidens and cheating creditors, in contracting enormous debts and in boasting of their remaining unpaid; nor was this demoralisation confined to private life. The cabinet of Versailles,

in its treatment of all the European powers, followed
the rules of this modern philosophy . . . it treated laws
treaties and truth with contempt, and ever insisted upon
its own infallibility. The doctrine that a prince can do
no wrong had a magical effect upon the other sovereigns
of Europe. Louis XIV became their model, and the object
to which most of them aspired, the attainment like him
of deification on earth. Even Germany, impoverished and
weakened by her recent struggle, was infected by this
universal mania. In 1656 John George II began to act
the part of a miniature Louis XIV in starving and desolate
Saxony. . . . To him succeeded in 1680 John George III
who spent all he possessed on his troops; then in 1691
John George IV who reigned until 1694 and whose mis-
tress reigned jointly with her mother over the country
and plundered the people, whilst his minister openly carried on a system of robbery and extortion.'[1]

And so we arrive at Bach's own Germany in Bach's
own time, with the ruling class definitely anti-popular
and anti-Christian, and as definitely hand in glove with
the ecclesiastical class.

The varying alignments of the French monarchy and
the sub-divisions of the German Empire, and the opposition between Roman and Lutheran ecclesiasticisms,
are confused and almost unintelligible unless we realise
that the masses of the people were opposed in some instances to a Catholic aristocracy with feudal connections,
and in other cases to a Protestant bourgeoisie which,
with increasing financial power, was beginning to as-
sume aristocratic airs.

[1] Menzel, *History*, cited, chap. CCXXI.

The religion and the political bias of the governing class of Germany were dictated by a will to keep their own people in subjection, and by a struggle to maintain, and if possible to extend, their powers and possessions against their own peers, and especially against the growing pretensions of the commercial class. Wherever feudal influence was deeply entrenched the Roman Catholic organization was favoured. It had served the feudal purpose while it played the game of betraying the Christian principles which had made it popular from the beginning; and it could still function treacherously in so far as the ignorant and superstitious masses were concerned.

There was one outstanding exception—feudal Prussia, where it suited the purpose of the Brandenburgers to be associated with the rising influence of commerce and finance.

Of Protestant declaration there were two kinds: the one Orthodox Lutheran, the other Pietist. These were the respective expressions in theological terms of the growing commercial interests, and of those who were on the side of the artisans and peasantry.

As we know from the story of the Reformation in England, full power and influence did not at once pass from men of feudal and Catholic faith to men of mercantile and Protestant faith. They struggled against each other for power, but had in fact to learn to share it between them until such time as they became merged in one ruling class. Quite early in the struggle rich families of middle-class origin gave financial backing to the 'Holy' Roman Empire.

Even in Thuringia, 'the headquarters of the Protestant movement,' the old faith had a strong backing; and, as we shall see presently, affected the course of Bach's mental development. The difficulty was for the Protestant ecclesiastics to provide a religion which would ensure support from the ruling class without alienating the feelings of the masses who provided the driving power of the Reformation.

In the South, where Catholic influences were strongest, there still prevailed the habits which regularly accompany the division of a people into classes of extreme wealth and penury, and as regularly lead to some kind of popular revolt.

'Licence was carried to the greatest excess in Baden-Durlach where the margrave, Charles William, built Carlsruhe in the midst of forests, A.D. 1715, and in imitation of the celebrated French deer parks. There he kept a hundred and sixty garden nymphs who bore him a countless number of children.'

In order to compete with so accommodating a religion as the decadent Roman Catholic, Protestant theologians had to be even more accommodating. But where solid interests were at stake the particular brand of religion did not matter very much. The Elector of Saxony, whose influence was paramount in Bach's country and early life, changed from Protestant to Catholic that he might succeed to the throne of Poland; and the reader may be reminded that, according to the arrangement made by Roman and Lutheran princes and priests assembled at Augsburg, it was decided that the religion of the peoples of Germany should be that of their various rulers. Presumably, therefore, they were to change when the local kinglet changed!

For a sceptical ruling class such changes meant nothing. For the people they were vital.

Abstract and obscure though the theology seems to us, the vague phrases really referred to things of material importance. People were in some ways more superstitious than their fathers had been [1] but anyhow their Protestantism had definite relation to their physical well-being and mental freedom. They may have been puzzled to explain what they were talking about when they cursed 'the scarlet woman of Babylon' and pinned their faith to 'the New Jerusalem'; but they knew well enough what they suffered because of the gaily living women on whose account their princes taxed them dry; and with all of the life and hope that remained to them they looked for a better state of affairs in the future.

It seems to have been those of the popular party with the most realistic ideas who had given Luther most

[1] For Protestant superstitions at the time of the Reformation see *The Literary Remains of Dürer.*

trouble—whose pressure made him eventually as big a reactionary as any Catholic. It was not until Protestantism had been promoted as 'more advantageous for princes' that the official leader of the Reformation felt sure of his own position; for he was attacked, not only by those who looked to Rome and Paris for leadership and instruction, but also by those Germans who wanted a reform of the ecclesiastical organization indeed, but Christian conditions of life as well. Even after he had accommodated his doctrine to the will of the princes who professed Protestantism, many of those princes continued to accept French cash for the betrayal of their own people; and it was a common thing for them to sell thousands of their subjects as cannon-fodder to England, Holland, and other powers.

Such a religion was Protestant only in name; and when it settled down, in its turn, into a dangerous and oppressive organization, there arose the sect called Pietists—a sort of Methodists—to recall once again the essential values of Christianity.

Bach called himself orthodox, and outwardly allied himself with the anti-Pietists of his time. So doing he deserted the tradition of his family; but his art gave the lie to his religious professions. He was of course bothered by the puritanical element in Pietism, because it sought to banish beauty as well as badness. Dr Sanford Terry well expresses it: 'Bach's genius, as his music reveals it, . . . and his simple piety had much in common with a school of religion which put faith before formalism, though he deplored the puritan severity which ruled out art from the adornments of the sanctuary.' [1]

Bach had to earn a living in the only way known to him. The means were in the hands of his spiritual enemies. He acted much as Michael Angelo and Rabelais acted in the like case; but because Bach's material was music the insurrectionary nature of his symbolism is less obvious.

[1] Sanford Terry, *Bach: a Biography*, p. 82.

Chapter Three

CHRISTIAN OR LUTHERAN?

BACH was brought up in the hard school of realism.

He was born at Eisenach on March the twenty-first, 1685. That was the birth year of Handel also; of Gay too, the author of the Beggars' Opera; and of Berkeley, the English bishop with the atheistic philosophy. The Pope was Innocent XI, 'a man of whom even his enemies found it hard to speak evil'—a Pope who allied himself with Protestant powers in order to check the pretensions of the Catholic king, Louis XIV. That is one of many things which go to prove that the theological strife of creeds was but a small matter as compared with the economic strife which lay at the root of the changing conditions.

Louis was then at the climax of his autocratic power. Thousands of Protestants were being massacred in France; thousands more sought refuge in countries where there was less intolerance.

It was a time of architectural lavishness and inanity; a time when painting and literature were becoming ex-

Reproduced by courtesy of the publishers, from Johann Sebastian Bach
by C. Hubert H. Parry, G. P. Putnam's Sons

BACH'S BIRTHPLACE IN EISENACH

hausted for lack of freedom of thought, and only music remained as a possibly true expression.

Bach's mother died when he was nine years old; his father a year later. He then went to live with an older brother who was also a musician; but it proved no satisfactory home for him.

One of the first evidences of his passion for music was the stealthy copying by moonlight of a coveted book of manuscript. The copy he made, it is said, was taken from him.

At the age of fifteen he left his brother and joined the choir of St Michael's convent at Lüneberg. It was the action of a youth with an eye to the main chance. That particular choir was a goal desired of many boys. Not only was there in its library a particularly wide range of music, but its organization was such that individual earnings were possible.

Bach's ancestors had been gildsmen, town musicians, municipal personages of varying distinction; and had been known over a large part of Germany as musical craftsmen of great skill. With the suppression of the gilds had come a great change. German musicians could no longer organize themselves upon a communal basis: they must now take service with princeling, with Council of Burgher-notables, or with whatever religious organization had been able to adapt itself to the new conditions. The convent of St Michael's was among the religious foundations which had managed to retain a good deal of its endowments by suiting itself to the requirements of Lutheranism; and it continued even as an evangelical establishment until its dissolution in 1850.

There Bach probably found the kind of sheltered life he needed if he were properly to educate his musical nature. His voice did not last long; when it broke he made himself indispensable to the convent authorities as a fiddler.

So things went for three years, the youngster making the best use of his time—tramping long distances to hear distinguished organists in other places, developing his own skill as a contrapuntist both on paper and on the organ.

We must bear in mind that it was at first his intention to be an executive musician. It accounts for some of the showy passages in his earlier compositions. The facility engendered placed him at a great advantage when, later on, his power as a composer ripened. It is only in these latter days that a composer is expected to achieve good work without a personal mastery over musical instruments and immediate and continuous relation with the public.

In Bach's day the chief musical bond between the musical artist and the masses of the public was the hymn-tune; but the hymn-tune was not then, as now, a dull and ponderous music, with steam-roller organs lugging congregations along monotonous roads. The hymn-tune of Bach's day, the chorale, was immediately derived from the songs of the people themselves. Sturdy it certainly was, with the sturdiness of German character; but it had not quite lost the dancing legs of folk-music.

Gevaert was of the opinion that in the earliest years of the Christian era sacred songs were adapted to pagan tunes picked up in the streets of Rome. It seems not unlikely, for that kind of musical piracy has generally taken place when a popular cause has found itself with ideas but without songs. Under such circumstances suitable words have generally been written for tunes already well known. Modern examples within our knowledge include the songs of political parties and the Salvation Army.

Embarrassing situations have sometimes resulted from that procedure; and we are not surprised when we learn that there were protests in the early Christian Church because of the origin and associations of some of the music. The fact that a tune is used with new words does not always ensure the oblivion of the old ones. Accordingly objections were lodged from time to time because certain tunes raised unsuitable thoughts in the minds of the worshippers. St Jerome, Pope Marcellus, and Walther the Lutheran hymnologist, each in his time had occasion to purge sacred songs from awkward secular associations. For the greater part, however, the raids of holy men upon unholy quarters for their popular tunes proved successful. Without popular expression in song there can be no real mass expression of feeling. Mass expression of feeling is necessary if men are to win full courage of their faith. Without such expression faith seems personal and isolated, and the faithful are timid accordingly.

On the other hand, attempts to change, curb, or divert mass expression in music have been made when it has been desired to modify or damp down a faith. So it was when Gregory the Great suppressed the Ambrosian congregational songs. So it was when Marcellus bade Palestrina and his fellow composers eliminate from their masses the slight connections with popular song that still remained. So it was when Luther in his later and reactionary mood advised the preservation of an elaborate scholastic art, as distinct from the congregational hymns preferred by the militants of the Reformation.

What Pope Gregory failed to effect proved far beyond Luther's power; and the German Christians stuck to the principle of congregational song as long as their struggles were hopefully maintained. As we shall see presently, Bach got into trouble on that very account. What happened when heart for the fight had been lost will also be seen.

Luther finally effected a sort of compromise. He was quite unsympathetic with the communal spirit which gave real impetus to the Reformation, though it was the original spirit of Christianity itself. Luther's own character, and his awareness of the commercial forces working for the Protestant opportunists, were amusingly revealed by his appeal to the civil authorities that a publisher should be prevented from pirating his theological writings. However, he was also a shrewd politician, and knew how to offer an apparent concession to the public, while retaining real power in his own hands. It was that sort of action which he took in the matter of the Reformation hymns. Many of them he took from the Gregorian tradition, taking care that the tunes were modified when necessary to bring them into line with the popular idea of a good melody. Other tunes were gathered from secular and foreign sources. Some were specially composed, Luther taking a hand in that job also. At the same time he put a check upon the popular share in church music, by maintaining certain art forms which were beyond the popular understanding—art forms of undoubted beauty, and originally derived from the evolved polyphonic sense of the people themselves. But that had flourished three hundred years earlier. In Luther's time all such art was derived from a cultural life removed from, and sometimes opposed to, the needs of the masses of the people.

The great Reformist's own political development explains the musical compromise. So long as he needed the support of the masses who were in revolt to ensure the propagation of his theological ideas, so long did he adopt a popular attitude, and admitted the folk-song as the basis for religious music. But when his political position had been modified to gain the support of the German princes against the Papacy he modified his artistic plans also, and admitted into the reformed church service the uncommon forms of leisure-class art.

Under happier conditions of life for the common folk such an attitude would have been justifiable. Luther's own enthusiasm for music was genuine enough, and he had real love for, and understanding of, elaborate polyphony. As Bach's finest interpreter says, Luther's appreciation of polyphonic music remains the best statement of the case to this very day: 'This is most singular and astonishing, that one man sings a simple tune or tenor as musicians call it, together with which three, four, or five voices also sing, which as it were play and skip delightfully round this simple tune or tenor, and wonderfully grace and adorn the said tune with manifold devices and sounds, performing as it were a heavenly dance.'[1]

Unfortunately it was the same man who said, 'Singing is the best exercise there is. We have nothing else at all comparable with it. I am very glad that God has denied to these obstinate rebels of peasants a gift so valuable, so full of consolation. They do not care for music, and they reject the word of God.'[2] For it was

[1] Quoted from Schweitzer's *Bach*, Eng. transl., I, 29.
[2] Michelet, *Life of Luther*, Eng. transl., (Bohn's Library), p. 288.

in fact those same 'obstinate rebels of peasants' who were responsible, not only for many fine tunes, but for the driving force of the Reformation itself.

The real musical expression of what remained of Christianity in Germany in the sixteenth century was not to be found in its cultured art, but in its popular religious songs. Schweitzer declares that the popular poetry is incomparable of its kind: 'Before it even the splendour of the Psalter pales.' The Protestant hymns carried with them one of the truest signs of a vital art in their immediate relation to the events of the day.

People with plenty of spare time can make art-works for beauty's sake; but the art that is made or strongly approved by a great body of people will have an expressional force which in the long run will influence even the tendency of leisure-class art. Whether that influence is good or bad will be dictated by the material conditions of the people.

Of that fact the most interesting example in our own day is the influence which the songs of the American negroes have had upon every branch of music. From it have developed not only music-hall songs and ball-room dances, but a great part of the activity of Stravinsky and his like. The speeding-up of modern industry, with its nervous reactions upon the human organization, finds due and natural expression in such music.

In earlier and less hurried times popular influence

was equally powerful and much less tortured. It was the common people's predilection for wood as a material for building which determined the most beautiful and characteristic form of the English dwelling house. [1] It was the method and style of the artisan painters of the Middle Ages which enabled Dante Gabriel Rossetti, Burne-Jones and others to make an end of the petty bourgeois ideals of Victorian art. In the same way renewed life has periodically been given to verse by harking back to the form of the folk ballad. Thus also the popular German songs of the fifteenth and sixteenth centuries became the substructure of the greatest music the world has yet known.

We are already aware that Bach was an orthodox Lutheran, and opposed to the so-called Pietism of some of the sincerest Christians of his time; and in a certain external sense the master actually halted at the point where Lutheranism had halted. The forms of both doctrine and music were such that the uneducated masses were necessarily excluded from full understanding and appreciation. The dogmas of the theologians were but dark shadows of the real and popular interpretation of Christianity. It was of little use to maintain the right to use pet allegories, if the rights of real life were to be lost in the struggle. It was of little use to win the right to partake of the sacrament in both kinds —and that was one of the major issues in theological

[1] Shaw Sparrow. *The English House*, pp. 60-1.

terminology—if the people could not also maintain their right to the bread of labour and the wine of joy. It was of little use to demolish the idol of a holy mother over the church door, if they were unable to demolish the idolatry which made motherhood unholy at their domestic hearths and in the seraglios of their masters.

So far as Bach was conscious of his religion in intellectual and dogmatic terms he halted where Lutheranism halted. Notwithstanding his sturdy stand for artistic freedom, he seems to have had no idea of the need for general and material civic freedom—conditions of reality without which artistic and religious freedoms are but shadows.

But there is in the nature of real art a curious dependence upon the finest common feeling of its time. Ideas couched in abstract terms by clericals and other intellectuals are conceivable by the masses only in real values and active forms. Art cannot issue from abstractions, it is clear, but from the realities which only yield the necessary emotion.

So Bach was forced subconsciously to express in music many ideas towards which he professed antagonism in real life.

Discouragement fell upon the German masses as a consequence of the Lutheran compromise; and the degree of discouragement defined the point at which the congregational spirit ceased to express itself creatively through ecclesiastical channels. So long as the people believed that Luther and his successors alluded to practical Christian conditions and behaviour, their hymns were sung by the whole body of the congregation; but as the treachery became more and more obvious, the songs were less hearty, and so the use of the organ became a sign of declining faith.

Protestant music was then changing from an art of religious reality to an art of mere æsthetic beauty; though when Bach was engaged in the work a wonderful core of true religious expression remained, even if hidden in the remote terms of tonal symbolism.

The transition from music as religion to music as art may be followed through the greater part of Bach's own career. The master was always hovering between the possibilities of a music which was the highest expression of real life, and a music which had no other justification than its own superb logic. At one time he revealed a point of view identical with that of the masses of earnest Christians, at another time he would spread himself in a world of pure beauty where it was impossible for the uncultured masses to follow him.

The mere service of beauty is without inspiration; it was an innate sense of truth which enabled him to develop his musical ideas. From these ideas even his secular works were indirectly derived. Of that we have proof. He could very readily find the right and full expression for ideas which were characteristic of the pietist (the extreme left) point of view. He would even introduce hints of such into the music, though the libretto had given no suggestion of them. But when he set out to give musical clothing to words expressive of orthodox Roman doctrine or the official Lutheran reaction, his creative spirit failed to be kindled, and he had to dish up music already composed, derived from an authentic emotion. This was the case even for one of the works which is regarded as among his greatest, the Mass in B minor. That is another aspect of the spiritual tragedy of the master's life.

By means of the chorale, the Christian song of Christian people in an unchristian age, Bach concentrated and voiced what was noblest in that age. It was a thing from which he could not escape if he were to have any real life as an artist, or any self-respect as a church worker.

His earliest compositions date from his student years at Lüneberg. They are all organ studies based upon chorales.

When later on he attempted to compose hymn-tunes of his own he failed, and produced instead sacred songs showing traces of a mixed parentage—being partly German folk-song, partly formal aria. But when he took the tunes which had already been made by the genius, or sealed with the approval, of the German people— when upon them he brought to bear his ready sympathy as artist and wonderful skill as craftsman—there ensued an artistic development of the noblest kind, even though it was veiled by a double symbolism. First there was the verbal symbolism of the theologians, and then the analogical symbolism of the music. The ideas which reached expression in that remote, almost secret fashion, corresponded the more truly with the lives of the people themselves, hindered as they were by a double obstacle—the refusal of Christian behaviour by their secular masters, and the darkening of Christian theory by the ecclesiastics.

Lutheranism had failed to recreate Christianity in the material terms of the thirteenth century; so people's thoughts turned inward to find in hopes and dreams what was denied in real life. Their hopes were sick with long deference. Their dreams were confused with clerical distortion.

So the problem faced by the youthful Bach at his desk in St Michael's convent at Lüneberg was not only a problem to be solved by contrapuntal skill and familiarity with fingerboard; it was also the more wonderful and spiritual problem of finding the right expression for those deferred hopes, and a satisfactory and clarifying interpretation of those confused dreams.

In Bach's Lüneberg variations upon 'Christ, der du bist der helle Tag,'[1] there are strange musical clues to ideas impossible of verbal statement; or when possible,

[1] Novello Edition, Bk. XIX, 36; Peter's Ed., V, 60.

opposed in spirit to the interpretation proposed by orthodox theologians and their masters. The first verse

> Lord Christ, thou art the heavenly light
> Who dost disperse the shades of night
> All radiant Thou, the Father's Son
> Dost spread the brightness of His throne.

has for its setting a straightforward statement of the tune.

For the second verse

> O dearest Lord, e'er guard our sleep
> From foes' assaults our slumbers keep;
> And let us find in thee our rest,
> Nor be by Satan's wiles oppressed.

Bach devised a double idea: in the upper part a prayerful music, as if asking for divine guard, and the gracious answer to the prayer; in the lower part a sinuous figure for the wily Satan.

Noticeable details are the emphasis on the thought of security in the sevenfold repetition of the monotone crochets in the fourth phrase of the tune; and the deliciously naive cadence wherein the composer figured victory, the soul rising to its peace, the serpent sinking into the abyss. That is the sort of realistic detail of which Bach's music is full. It is the external feature which, more than any other, proclaims the identity of his religious and artistic nature with that of the Middle Ages.

We cannot but understand from the facts recalled

in the previous chapter what were the Satanic wiles which oppressed Bach's fellow Christians. But to have referred to the hundred and sixty garden nymphs of a Catholic prince as daughters of Satan, or to have referred to the extortions of the princes who were aping the Grand Monarch as the assaults of foes, was impossible. In the pregnant phrase of William Blake, it was an age when 'the gate of the tongue was closed.' The greater need, therefore, for a music which should open a secret gate, and by whatever peep of reality it could give, salve and quicken the bludgeoned human spirit. Through such a gate could pass many ideas which were censored even by the clericals who had been originally established to circulate them.

Equally realistic is a figure in the third verse:

> E'en though our weary eyelids fall,
> O keep our hearts true to thy call.
> Above us stretch thy sheltering hand
> Lest sin or shame our dreams should brand.

When the composer had pictured the falling eyelids of the first line, he turned the phrase round into a rising passage, and so suggested the idea of alertness. He did not disdain a physical suggestion also for the stretched hand, expressing it by a straining syncopation; and he gave the upsurgence of sin and shame in a passage which throws the listener's thoughts back to the previous variation, as if to indicate that though the devil had been thrown down at the end of the second verse he was still capable of returning.

And in the fourth verse the fiend does very surely return, not only in the words, but more powerfully in the music. The verse runs

> We pray Thee, Jesus Christ our Lord,
> 'Gainst Satan's cunning help afford.
> May he whose fell hosts camp around
> Ne'er drag us with him to the ground.

The music makes it clear that the outcome of the strife is by no means certain. From beginning to end the tune is merged in the serpentine figures which symbolise the Satanic hosts.

In the earlier years of Gothic growth, when the fight was still undecided, pictures of The Last Judgment had been painted upon the interior walls of churches, generally across the arch which spanned the steps to the chancel. It was 'the most prominent place on the whole of the church walls.' The artisan painters of that time seemed to have been as much concerned with devils gobbling up sinners as with the bliss of the good people.[1] But when, later on, the people gained more influence in governmental organization, and consequently enjoyed a better material life on earth, the victory over Satan seemed so certain that there was the less need to press home the results of wickedness.

[1] Frank Kendon, *Mural Paintings in English Churches during the Middle Ages.*

Consequently, in later representations the artists were more concerned to show the saints. 'Wells, Westminster, and Lincoln manifest the joys only. There is almost a merriment in this thirteenth century delivery of the sculptural mind.'[1]

Lest any wiseacre disputes this on the ground that the difference was national, let the reader remember the essentially international basis of medieval Christianity. The return of the devils in the music of Bach had no exact counterpart in the art of England, it is true; but that was because the composers of the Elizabethan decadence and the Restoration shame were not even religious enough to be ashamed of, or disgusted with them. Purcell's devils had no teeth for the same reason that Michel Angelo's angels had no wings. Bach, with a more realistic and topical feeling for religious ideas, knew that deviltry had resumed its sway on earth, and was therefore obliged, as a conscientious artist, to place it in the forefront of his music. It is a thought which was often with him, and we shall meet with even more significant expressions of it.[2]

For the fifth variation a symbolism is used akin to that of illuminated manuscripts and the illustrative comment of William Blake.[3]

[1] Prior, *Eight Chapters*, etc., already cited.
[2] For example the 5th number of *Ein Feste Burg*.
[3] For a good interpretation of the latter see Wicksteed's *Study of Blake's Book of Job*.

The words run:

> Sure 'tis thy heart's most precious blood
> Has won our souls thy brotherhood;
> And so indeed the Father meant
> When to the earth Thyself He sent.

During periods of revolt the feeling of brotherhood is a key-emotion, and not approved by the powers in possession. Its implications are nearer to action than to art. Nevertheless, Bach, boy though he still was, found for the idea an obscure but fitting symbol—indeed, perhaps the more to his purpose because obscure.

The tune is placed in the tenor and written in such a manner that both hands of the performer must be employed in its delivery, so there is no possibility of the main theme being brought into prominence by means of a solo stop. The melody is, in fact, entirely merged in the figure which plays around it from beginning to end, even as the Christian idea of the brotherhood of all human beings centred around the typical Man, the Son of the All-Father.

A more physical realism returns in the fifth verse:

> O set thine angels round our bed,
> And let our thoughts to thee be led,
> That guarded so—north, east, south, west,
> From Satan's lures we find sure rest.

Here the complete tune is set about with a waving wing-figure in triple time—the kind of figure which Bach generally associated with angels.

Hitherto the music has contained no part for the pedals of the organ. Such a part he added at a later date to the music of the last verse, where the chief thought is the all-sustaining power of God.

> Safe in Thy care so shall we sleep
> While wakeful angels watch do keep.
> O God eternal Three in One
> For ever may Thy praises run!

The reference to angels is musically translated into a rhythmic figure of four semi-quavers which seems a variation of the triple figure in the previous verse. The idea of the Trinity is represented by a triple statement of the crochet monotones which gave a hint of divine security to the emotion of the second verse.

The outstanding feature of these hymn-tune variations is, of course, the childlike realism of the thematic material. To musicians sophisticated with the knowledge of later, subtler, and less exuberant art-forms such realism may seem foolish, because the pictorial suggestiveness of music is limited, and secondary to its power of emotional evocation. Indeed the average music-lover with little opportunity for detailed study of the music would probably miss most of the symbolism, catching at a first hearing only the angel-figures and perhaps the Satanic allusions. But every detail was present for Bach himself, and that was in a way the chief thing, much as the wealth of scarcely visible figure-sculpture in Gothic had for its chief value, not the pleasure of the onlooker but the faith of the masons who carved it.

And if the realistic and remote symbols are lost in the general emotion of the music it must be remembered that the sculptural details of the twelfth and thirteenth centuries were none the less separately meaningful because they were secondary to the statement and dissemination of definite religious ideas.

Realism of sculptural detail was inevitable because the masons had a very present conception of religion and an increasing sense of the reality of Christianity; Bach's realism was due to the same cause, even though Christianity itself was in decline.

Whenever men are intent on the expression of thoughts which are material to their welfare, far from a pedantic attempt to divest their work of realistic suggestion, they will most certainly use any methods which give completest reality to their conceptions. They will not say, The idea of remorse is too subtle to be expressed in stone, which demands treatment in three-dimensional form. They will say, What physical suffering gives an expression nearest to that of remorse? and proceed to carve a figure like the grotesque on the tower of St. Michael's at Coventry, tearing its cheeks apart with its hands. If they cannot believe in the accepted religion of their time they will ignore it as Richard Strauss did, when he transferred his worship from the baby in the manger to the baby in the bath.

Not a matter of high thought, but at least of real thought; and a degenerate age can expect little high thought in its art. However puerile the matter of Strauss's Domestic Symphony it had the virtue of reality.

Only when men are pretending to give expression to ideas in which they do not believe do they make esthetic fuss, bothering their minds and confusing the art-lover with the rights and wrongs of movement suggested in stone, or fact in music. Only when artists have lost faith in life itself, and are bereft of any public cause worthy their service, do they regard topical and local and personal allusions as being in bad taste.

So with Bach.

The Christian struggle, which for most of us to-day is a matter of hypocritical pretence or scientific scepticism, was as real for Bach as for the medieval mason of Coventry—as real as the knowledge Strauss had of his own domestic life. Bach could no more avoid details of realism in his musical language than the craftsmen of the cathedral building could help referring to common details of their own preservation and knowledge, things generally concerning their civic lives as members of the international Christian brotherhood.

That Bach incorporated many petty and pregnant details in the great line of his work is another proof that he was most intent on expressing the realities of religion, and less concerned in making great works of art.

A thorough believer in anything will give expression to his belief with all the skill at his command, not with the idea of drawing attention to that skill, but with the intention of propagating his faith; nor will he pride himself on the small number of those who are able to receive his message. An artist of that kind will gain power with every effort that he makes, and sooner or later, if his cause is good and his industry unfailing, he will become in his own particular medium what is called 'a great artist.' But a man who sets out to be a great artist and has no cause to serve, can never become more than a clever juggler; we may admire him for his trickery, but that will soon tire us, and we shall feel the need of a fresh diversion.

The fact that in his early hymn-tone variations Bach had felt the need of expressing his thought in such vivid detail is sign enough that his purpose was not that of mere music-making. Cleverest of all music makers he certainly became; that was because he wholeheartedly served by means of music the most vital principles of the civilization in which he had been born; so that, even now, when we no longer believe the legends which enabled that civilization to be established, we are still held by this music—this music which is full of childish conceits, and yet reaches the noblest expression of human feeling ever conveyed by such means.

For some reason or other Schweitzer, and following him Sanford Terry, fail to recognize that the Lüneberg

Variations express the successive stanzas of the hymn. That is the more strange as it was Schweitzer who most completely revealed the pictorial tendencies of Bach's music, and wrote of 'the serpentine lines that contort themselves at the mention of the word Satan; the charming flowing motives that enter when angels are mentioned.'

During the whole of his working life Bach used just such a realistic phraseology, combined of course with the more essential architectonic and emotional forms of musical art.

More than that: from the outset of his career he seems to have developed a kind of secret code with which to express ideas not generally acceptable to the prevailing opinion of his time. Dante in his 'Divine Comedy,' Goya in his 'Caprichios and Disparates,' and Blake in his pictures and prophetic books, took similar courses; but the difficulty we have in arriving at the true thoughts of the latter, for lack of keys to their codes, much confuses our appreciation of their work. Bach, like Dante, is more easily to be enjoyed by us. Even without an understanding of the references with which their works abound— even the secular and lighter works—the arts of the poet and the musician are such that we can easily enjoy the great emotional and architectural splendour which enshrines the detail.

Such details were almost certainly employed instinctively, or imitatively, by the young musician. It could

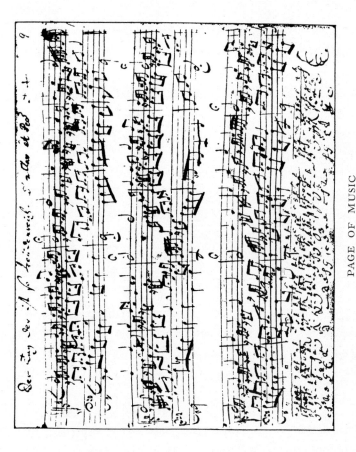

PAGE OF MUSIC

Facsimile of Chorale "Der Tag der ist so freudenreich"

have been only later, when he had been angered by the treachery of Christian officialdom that he consciously applied a realistic mood at once vivid and concealed.

So far as I have been able to analyse his music, Bach seems to employ three kinds of artistic realism—all of them to be found in the Lüneberg Variations.

The first is a direct realism such as anyone might easily recognise and accept: the sinuous figure for the serpentine devil who seduced Mother Eve, the little drooping figure for weary eyelids, and so on.

The second is an arbitrary realism which, suitably enough, is used for the musical exposition of theological dogmas: the idea of the Trinity as represented in the last Lüneberg Variation. Abstruse allegories of that kind are scarcely to be generally understood unless their intention has been previously stated. Folk with a very clear idea of what they mean by the Trinity may reap special satisfaction from that last variation, for example; but the average person, I think, will be inclined to smile.

The third, and in some ways the most important kind of realism, is in some sort withheld by symbolism such as we found in the fifth variation analysed above. It is a musical analogue of the symbolism used by Goethe when he represented the opposition between established power and libertarian effort by the symbols of Zeus and Prometheus, whereas the majority of people of his time would have more readily understood him if he had used the symbols in current use, Jehovah and Jesus; but, of course, the use of the latter symbols would have betrayed the mental leanings which he then wished to disguise. Bach was in a similar plight; and, for that very reason, his realism when darkened by such symbolism, is generally the most important for our study, because it veils the statement of an idea which could only be made if it were hidden at the very moment of utterance.

Consider the idea symbolised in the fifth variation of 'Christ der du bist der helle Tag', the idea that the son of God became man that all men might be shown how to become sons of God. That in plain language can only signify that there is no real difference between the idea of God and the idea of a fully developed human being. Moreover, it places the idea of development, of education, in a social light: we understand that there can be no such thing as a proper development of human faculty unless it is based on the idea of human brotherhood, of equality in matters of material need.

From that follows an understanding of the joyous possibilities of what is naturally unequal in human beings; for the things which are peculiar to persons are often the things with which they are able to enrich the world.

Such an idea would have met with as much, perhaps with more derision in Bach's time than in our own; so he darkened the realism of the thought by means of a comparatively obscure symbolism.

What was Bach's position?

The degenerate Roman and Lutheran theologians continued to use Christian phrases for the maintenance of their own material power. They do so to this day. To refrain from such use would even now send them toppling; and in Bach's day the Pietist movement was a much more real thing than any leftward sect among present day churches.

Nevertheless such power obviously depends upon the suppression of the facts of brotherhood and equality. Political organizations suppress them by force; their ecclesiastical arms subvert the very ideas by twisting words. Indeed the words of the above-quoted hymn were designed to suggest a mystical brotherhood between Christ in the skies and men on earth; and so to undermine the real meaning of brotherhood as the right to *material* equality between Pope and swineherd, Luther and Zwingli, the Duke of Weimar and a member of his band. That was the reality of Christian ethic which the anti-Christian churches were destroying in Christ's name.

What could a mere boy-musician do under those circumstances?

It was clearly impossible for any natural emotion to be evoked by the idea of brotherhood between a man and a god. It was hard enough to conceive such an idea as between master and man, as the tone of all contemporary writing shows.

How could Bach find music for an emotion which could not arise?

What he did was to ignore the theological trickery, and pick up the original symbolism of Christian religion at the time of its most glorious reality, writing a fragment wherein a coherent but inaudible tune proclaimed the idea of Christ the symbol of perfect manhood, while audible figuration declared that whether you were treble, alto, or bass, you were equal in the world where the central song was a statement of brotherhood.

Using the least material of the arts, and living in a world of thought and dream, Bach at once discovered to his hand methods of realistic expression most suitable for the preservation of ideas opposed to the main current of the external world.

The other arts had ceased to function as Christian activities. No real Christian architecture was possible in a world where material power was in the hands of anti-Christians. For them the dull piles and vulgar artificialities of the Renaissance, with its pseudo-pagan pretences.

No real Christian paintings could be set up in public places. Even in Dürer's time, two hundred years earlier, the typical madonna and child had left the stable and apparently leased a palace with park complete.[1]

No real Christian literature was possible; the nearest approach to such a thing was a hymnology with a remote and treacherous heaven-when-you-die symbolism. The true literature of the time was the sceptical philosophy of Bishop Berkeley and the savage satire of Dean Swift.

Music with its limited and elusive relation to real things was the only art by means of which Christian truth might still be asserted; and even musicians were sick with the sorrow of lost reality, tending to feel and express pessimism in all that related to the real world, not uninclined to serve the romanticism which looked for a better world only after death.

Students of history are familiar with the phenomenon. When people have been disappointed of an improvement in their material conditions, and suffer such degradation and hardship as makes them question the basis of life itself, they incline to what seems to be the next best thing, and elaborate ideas of what should have been, telling of things that happen in strange places—Dante in his 'Paradiso,' More in his 'Utopia'; or foretelling things which must some day be in a better world, even for persons who suffer in the present—

[1] See, for examples, *The Virgin and Child* (Basle Museum) and *The Feast of Rose-garlands* (Imperial Gallery, Vienna); reproductions in Knackfuss' monograph on *Dürer*, translated by Campbell Dodgson.

Bunyan in 'Pilgrim's Progress,' Tolstoy in his metaphysical writings. When it is not prudent to propagate even such remote ideas of decent life, a yet more obscure method is chosen, and the real thought becomes clouded with plastic and literary symbols which confuse even more than they convey.

Music, however, is removed from the world of reality; at such times it receives the full charge of suppressed feeling, and takes on the most realistic forms of which it is capable.

I am not arguing that Bach was completely conscious of the role he was playing in the revolt against the decay of Christian principles of life. He was probably not yet fully conscious even of the realistic shapes which music took at his hands. He was not the first to develop those shapes. He just expressed himself in the most natural way; and because he had a mind already constituted and educated to face facts, the phrase-forms which arose in his mind had a factual quality.

The music which he thus made at the outset of his career was probably a written-out version of interludes to be played in church before the singing of the separate verses of the hymn. It seems to us a strange method of drawing out the church service to an unconscionable length; but that may be because the relation between divine service and human pleasure has now been lost.

As works of art the Lüneberg variations are monotonous; as works of religion we have no longer any use for them; even as organ-studies they are of little value because the pedals are not fairly employed.

Young Bach probably wrote them for an occasion when he was required to deputise at the instrument, and before his pedal-technic was equal to his imagination. One authority says that the pedal-part was written in later. If so it is an interesting example of the artist's restraint and sense of fitness, in that he added the pedals only to the last variation where its symbolic value is the more apt to express the mighty supporting hand of God. But the real quality of that boy of seventeen is best to be seen in his figurative imagination.

How came it that the organist in Bach's time had so assertive a position in the church service that he was allowed, and even instructed, to 'strike in' such long passages of instrumental music between the verses of congregational singing? Was the congregational so musically developed, and so glad to have its religious emotions subtilised by instrumental art, that the people were content and glad to pause and consider the beauties of such interludes as a fuller revelation of the more obvious meanings of the words?

For us the organ is a large noise to cover the shuffle of feet as the congregation enters or leaves church, or to drown the asthmatic voices of elderly people; or a soft noise to fill in the intervals of a ritual; or an anachronism. For Bach and the church-worshippers of his time the organ was not quite so unserviceable an instrument. Nevertheless it was largely used to cover up the rags of their poverty-stricken Christianity.

As lute and viols were introduced into the singing of decadent madrigalians, so the organ into the service of the Christian Church—at first to bolster up the increasing timidity of singers who had a diminishing polyphonic sense, and then to cover the shame of their general inefficiency and unbelief.

In Germany the contrapuntal style derived from the school of the Netherlands gave way before the monodic style derived from Italy, the headquarters of a Renaissance which was moribund from its birth; even as the polyphony of Gothic architecture in its aboriginal territory had given way before the pseudo-Hellenic and Imperial Roman forms of building fostered by the ruling classes in alliance with the Papacy.

At first lute, viols, and organ were used as crutches; but as the ability and feeling for free polyphonic tone lapsed in the decay of general culture, or were cast aside in favour of a monomelodic style, the meanness of the concerted tone became so pronounced that its fosterers were fain to mask it with a more decided and powerful sound. By means of the church-organ a cloak was thrown over the significant silences under and around the tunes.

It was not merely that singly uttered tunes were of lower esthetic value than the multitudinous life of the polyphonic style, though that must have been obvious

CHRISTIAN OR LUTHERAN?

enough. It was also that religious initiative had been beaten out of the hearts of the people, so that they no longer cared to sing, and in time lost the skill to do what once they could. If no instrument covered the weakness and the silence, there would have been little music of any kind, and the unreality of the religion exposed accordingly.

By degrees the organ of the fifteenth and sixteenth centuries had been developed to accompany music in the contrapuntal style, which was the first conception musicians had of part-music, until the point was reached when the instrument was more effective without than with the voices. So, from being an instrument of accompaniment it became an instrument of autocracy and suppression, the most domineering and unrelenting instrument in the history of music. It assumed control of the divine service in the same way that a steam-roller assumes control of the road-metal it crushes into equality without individuality.

Vulgarity of the most blatant kind has been reserved for the organs of our own day; but even in the eighteenth century the tendency was decided. Of course when an organist of talent is on the stool something interesting may be achieved under any circumstances; and Bach seems to have been about the last of a series of fine organists who made good musical commentary, even though some of them may have had little sympathy with the meaning of the service.

Our master went a step further than his predecessors; he made his commentary intense with real religious worship. But the situation was paradoxical: the greater master of a communal style in music wrote chiefly for the most autocratic of instruments! Of that more when we are considering his organ works as a whole.

The use of the organ for 'striking in' was not the most definite indication of congregational decadence. It even happened that the instrument was required *instead of* the singing, the organist making sole response to sentences of the priest. In this way it offered striking parallel to the reservation of the sacrament, one of the ostensible causes of the Lutheran rebellion itself! Or, to regard it from another angle, the mystic language of music without words took the place of that vulgar tongue which was yet another uncatholic item regarded as essential by Protestants.

When Bach left Lüneberg in 1703 it was in the hope of securing a position as organist at Sangerhausen. Thanks to Grand Ducal influence it was given to someone else. Instead of that he got a job as fiddler in the household of Duke Johann Ernst, a younger brother of the reigning prince.

The young duke seems to have been a pleasing and cultured person; but the musician made only a short stay there. It involved a servile and parasitical relationship which must have been hateful to any man with a sense of original creative power.

While fiddling in the band Bach was chiefly occupied with Italians forms of art—forms doubtless good in their origin, but, as encouraged by the ruling classes of Europe from that day to this, yet another means of obscuring the Christian principles which had informed the great and popular arts of the Middle Ages—the arts to which the nature of Bach was instinctively drawn.

Under such conditions the composer's creative impulse was not likely to receive stimulus, and it is significant that no works exist to testify to his inner life during those months.

Chapter Four

RESERVED RELIGION: REALISTIC ART

IN 1704 Bach was engaged as organist for the new church at Arnstadt, his first position of real responsibility. He was on active duty only three days a week. There naturally followed an immediate development of his faculty as composer. Before examining his works and what they signify of mental experience, let us try to sense the psychological atmosphere of the place.

Thuringia, though preponderantly Protestant, was no land of religious freedom. At the time of Bach's appointment there lived at Arnstadt John Frederick Treiber and John Philip, his son. The father was principal of the school whence Bach drew his choir-boys, and incidentally a great lover of music. The son was a considerable scholar; he had been connected with Jena University, but was compelled to leave on account of his religious views. Spitta says he was a freethinker, but does not indicate if the free thought took an atheistic turn, or merely showed a trend from the official and orthodox Reformist point of view.

We know how at all times the orthodox are inclined to stigmatise those who differ from them, even in a slight degree; and young Treiber's free thought may quite possibly have consisted merely of a mild criticism of current superstitions.

After his expulsion from Jena John Philip took to scientific experiment. For that he was imprisoned. Subsequently he lived at Arnstadt with his father, but was forced to leave owing to controversy with the local religious authorities. Then he joined the Roman Church, and was quickly promoted to a respectable position as a professor of jurisprudence.

That gives some idea of the religious atmosphere in which Bach found himself.

From a material point of view the organist's position seemed fairly good, Bach being allowed double the salary which had been given to the man he displaced; but it is clear that from the outset Bach was not at his ease there.

Two details in connection with the appointment itself throw light upon the early and continuous contempt with which Bach treated his Arnstadt employers—the summary dismissal of his predecessor, and the sources of his salary.

It cannot have been a poor congregation. They had recently raised money for their new organ, nearly one half of the sum being provided by a rich burgher who received in return a special vault in the church; but of Bach's salary less than one-third was paid from the funds of the church, another third being derived from the local beer tax, and (chief shame!) a greater third from a 'hospital' which maintained a number of old people.

The hospital had a chapel of its own, and it is said that 'Bach drew his thirty thalers for playing on the chapel organ'; but the document which states the amount of the salary and the duties of the organist makes no reference to the hospital except as a source of funds; nor is there to my knowledge any evidence that Bach played there—certainly not as a regular part of his duties.

The whole affair looks uncommonly like one of those misappropriation of charity funds which have been regular occurrences in all countries during the centuries of declining Christian principle.[1]

During the second year of his appointment Bach got leave of absence that he might visit Lübeck to hear the famous organist-composer, Buxtehude, and apparently to do something in the way of personal study there. Without further application Bach extended his four weeks' leave to nearly four months, missing even his Christmas duties at Arnstadt. After his return his explanations were, to put it mildly, so cavalierly expressed

---

[1] Dr. Terry half apologises for the sources of Bach's salary, saying that 'the church lacked funds'; but it is strange if a congregation of which a single member could subscribe 800 gulden for the organ, could not find one-tenth that sum by way of salary for the organist.

that one wonders whether he had meant to come back at all. In the northern town he must certainly have found himself in an atmosphere much more congenial to the active Protestantism which had always been a characteristic of the Bach family.

The first Bach mentioned by Spitta—Hans, alive in 1500—was chiefly memorable for protesting when the bourgeois council of Erfurt commandeered the communal mines; he got himself into prison, and was haled before the Catholic archbishop of Mainz, who was in league with the burghers. Veit Bach, whom John Sebastian looked upon as the chief of his forefathers, had migrated into Hungary, but returned to his Thuringian village that he might avoid the oppression of Jesuit rule and hold his faith in freedom. Hans was a miner, Veit a baker: both of the working class, there is no doubt of their tendency to interpret Christian doctrine in terms of their material lives. And though we find Bachs of a later time in such menial occupations as lackeys and capellmeisters (there was apparently little difference in the status of the two jobs, and in the case of one member of the family both kinds of service were required in the terms of his agreement with his employer), it is clear that the religious tradition of the whole family was on the Protestant and popular side.

With such a tradition behind him it would indeed be surprising if John Sebastian had not compared the more congenial atmosphere of Lübeck with the tyranny rampant at Arnstadt; and perhaps he stayed on at the northern town in the hope of finding there a permanent appointment for himself. He could probably have secured the reversion of Buxtehude's own post; but in that case he would have been expected to marry Buxtehude's daughter who was ten years his senior and no beauty. Evidence is not wanting that Bach was by way of falling in love with another girl at this very time.

One of the most important compositions of the Arnstadt period was an Easter Cantata. Spitta ascribes it to his first year there; but it seems rather likely that it dates from the weeks immediately following his return from Lübeck. It is not only influenced by the northern school of composers; it is also full of militant Protestant feeling, the libretto being couched in the extreme language reminiscent of the mystery plays of the Middle Ages.

Notwithstanding his traditions and personal leanings, Bach was a cautious and prudent person; and he would scarcely have written so militantly Protestant a work during his first year at Arnstadt—nor even during his second year, if he had not intended to risk the disapproval of his official superiors. Apart from the fact that he had seen how both Catholic and Lutheran officials were using their positions for other than religious ends, the case of young Treiber must have been very much before him. But his visit to Lübeck would have reinforced his natural feelings. Moreover, judging by the amusing independence of his tone when rebuked by his employers, it is clear that he had made up his mind to take other service at an early moment. The libretto of the Easter Cantata bears certain witness to that decision.

A matter which has not yet been properly studied is the reflection in Bach's compositions of the conditions and affairs of his private life. Musicians seem to have decided that his art had little to do with his life—that the external influences which can be traced in the cases of the majority of creative artists, are not noteworthy in the works of Bach. But it is remarkable how the librettos chosen, and in many cases perhaps written, by the composer, often seem to contain references, not only to local and topical things of Christian concern, but to incidents of his own personal career.

At first it may be thought rather far-fetched if I interpret passages in the Easter Cantata as signifying the discomfort of his life at Arnstadt, and his intention to leave at the earliest convenient moment. For example, the opening aria, 'Thou wilt not leave my soul in hell,' and the last line of all, 'I go my way rejoicing.' However, when it is discovered how many such coincidences there are in his works, the idea may seem more credible.

Such references are, of course, only incidental in the larger aesthetic and religious interpretation of the works. The real hell in which the souls of Christian people were suffering was the economic and military servitude which was being forced upon them; and the way of rejoicing was, theologically speaking, the way to a dream-world through the gate of the grave. The whole cantata is a Protestant pæan because Christ has shown his brothers how they may put from them the fear of death. The more personal element in the work is nearer the spirit of the Middle Ages. For us who, judging by our actions, believe neither in the international Catholicism of the twelfth and thirteenth centuries, nor the courageous Protestantism of the centuries which followed, nor even in the pious allegories of the Methodists in revolt against meaningless Orthodoxy, there seems little difference between the following from the York Mystery Play in which Jesus appears to Mary Magdalen after the Resurrection:

> All for joy melikes to sing.
> My heart is gladder than the glee;
> And all for joy of Thy rising
> That suffered death upon the tree.
> Of love now art Thou crowned King;
> There's none alive so true, so free.
> Thy love passes all earthly thing.
> Lord, blessed must Thou ever be!

and the following from Bach's Easter Cantata:

With sighs hell's complaining, earth's shouting for joy
Hell's moaning, earth's laughing, and knows no alloy;
For now is death robbed of his once boasted might;

My heart now rejoices to see the glad sight.
There see now! Deride him! Foul Satan's in flight!

The personal note in the two is indeed identical;
but there is between them the difference of a Christianity that has no fear of death, and a Christianity that
is desperately afraid even as it asserts immortality.

The Easter Cantata foreshadows the great Passions
which are as truly characteristic of an honest but decadent religion as the Christmas worship of Madonna
and Child had been characteristic of Christianity at its
noblest period. Since that period the masses of Christendom had suffered severely; and the Protestant point
of view was bound to emphasize, not the happiness of
birth, the glad glory of life, and the comparative unimportance of death, but the desperate hope of a victory
over death and a continuation of personality afterwards.
As it is expressed in this cantata:

He who did take on Him a mortal's bearing
As man hath crushed the foe our welfare that assailed;
And through His death His victory man is sharing
Immortal here I stand with Him.

Only by some such mystical belief could honest men
continue to hold Christian doctrines in face of the fact
that from the time of the Peasants' War until Bach's
own day thousands on thousands of Christians had perished rather than give up the effort to bring about the
Kingdom of Heaven upon earth. Hope was no longer

on earth; but a more desperate hope for a good time after death.

Someone has suggested that the Easter Cantata was composed to impress the local bigwigs who had rebuked Bach not only for his prolonged absence from duty, but for the style of his organ accompaniments to the hymns. They had charged him with making 'peculiar variations mingled with strange sounds whereby the congregation was confounded.' He was obliged to admit the former charge, but must have found it hard to swallow musical criticism from a class of men who are notoriously insensitive to musical ideas.

More amusing, and perhaps more valid, was the complaint lodged by one of the choir prefects, that Bach had at first made too much of the instrumental parts of the service, and then, when the superintendent had complained, had gone to the other extreme and made those parts inconveniently short. That kind of behaviour was not out of keeping with the composer's character.

Still more serious were the difficulties caused by the musician's inability to manage his choirboys, and his refusal to train them properly. He found it easier, and probably better from an artistic point of view, to compose choruses with elaborate under parts for adults who could read, and simple top lines—often melodies of hymns which were well known already—for the boys, rather than involve himself in treble parts which would need much rehearsal.

One cannot help smiling at the self-possession of the organist, and the curt answers he gave to his masters' questions—even regarding the occasion when he had descended to abusive words, and had even threatened to use his sword! In spite of all it is clear that the Consistory had much respect for their musician, great pride in possessing so distinguished a servant; and they were evidently disinclined to mete out to him the summary treatment his predecessor had experienced.

From the composer's point of view the Easter Cantata may in itself have seemed a sufficient justification for the French leave he had taken. It may even have been an indirect reply to the complaint regarding his hymn-accompaniments. It was typical of his nature, anyhow: if he might not develop his creative powers by elaborating the tunes in one way he would do so in another.

The time came when he took the words of hymns and set them to 'peculiar variations' throughout, with no hindrance in the way of congregational song until the very end.

In any case it is clear that Bach had made up his mind to let no routine of duty or official chiding hinder the main purpose of his life.

The supremely great artists of the world seem regularly to have found themselves in such a position. They have themselves been more or less aware of their own power—at first not so much in the capacity they have had to fulfil their artistic will, but rather in an all-compelling passion to perfect their skill, and then to reveal the reality of life as it has been presented to them. Dante and Shelley in their exile, Beethoven and Blake in the social repression of their lives, More and Bunyan in prison, were not more constrained than Bach would have been had he undertaken every detail of petty routine which was expected of him, and from a man of lesser creative instinct could fairly have been required.

For his employers at Arnstadt there is this much to be said: though they were annoyed they obviously had the feeling that some latitude should be accorded to their servant for the sake of his genius, or because of the glory which his service reflected on their church.

Bach himself, however, seems to have been unrelenting, and practically ignored those parts of the complaint against him which could not be easily adjudged in his favour. The fact seems to have been that his duties were crippling his growth as an artist, and were not even fulfilling a truly religious purpose.

Regular work with all it brings of security and discipline is one of the happiest things which life can offer to an artist; but there must be no element of humbug in the work—what is required of him must be what he can give without emotional repression or intellectual hypocrisy.

From the realistic nature of his creative activity it is

clear that Bach's mind was full of ideas which pertained to the contemporary life of Christians; but it was almost impossible for him to give free outlet to such ideas. He was no more free as an artist than young Treiber had been as a scientist.

The Reformation had been betrayed by those who had pretended to lead it. Lutheranism had become a mere badge of bourgeois respectability. The human imagination and capacity for realism which fused to visionary splendour in the musician's brain must have been frequently darkened when in touch with the pious pretences of his employers. The burgher-merchant not inaptly named Stomach, who got a vault on holy ground in exchange for his contribution to the organ-fund, was a much more important person in the Christian life of Arnstadt than the publican, the sinner, or the musician who had heaven and hell in his head.

So Bach's two years at Arnstadt were not notable for any great development of his power in the direct terms of vocal art. After the one outbreak in the Easter Cantata forms involving words were set aside; the time was then devoted to an extension of his skill as craftsman, especially in organ-playing and organ-composition.

He began to foreshadow some of the characteristics which were to prove his real individuality; and let it again be recalled that all individuality is of a superpersonal nature. Bach's business as a true artist was not to show how surprisingly different he was from other musicians; it was rather to prove by his manner that he was *not* divided from those of his predecessors and contemporaries whose aims and workmanship were good. Greater soul though he was, it was not his business to cultivate an uncommon style. That could be left to the arty persons who had only platitudes to babble. For Bach, who had the need to express serious common things which the majority of men were too weak or cowardly to express, the common musical tongue of his day was good enough. Of course, the very fact that he had bold and rebellious things to utter in a world where courage and revolt were uncommon caused him to use the common tongue in uncommon ways.

He began to do new things with the pedal of the organ, as in the third verse of the chorale-prelude, 'Wer nur den Lieben Gott'; and especially he continued to foster the intuitive impulse which, at such a time, finds in the art of music the truest and most effective form of religious worship. The spirit of the sincere artist might be revolted by the disgusting hypocrisy on all sides; but what was blasphemy in the mouths of money-grubbing burghers could be transferred into another atmosphere and given reality and ethereality in the remote and spiritual forms of wordless art.

Luther had handed over the religious conscience of the people to the haphazard and fickle care of their political rulers and economic controllers. Only a few years later than the period we are now considering the

Duke of Weimar openly forbade his subjects 'to reason under pain of correction.'[1] Young Treiber's case shows that such a tyrannical spirit already prevailed in Arnstadt; and now petty officialdom was beginning to interfere even with music.

The Consistory had decided that Bach's musical logic 'confounded the congregation.' So he was thrown back entirely upon his creative will as musician; and that sped him upon a path which resulted in the wonderful chorale-preludes, pieces wherein the music secretly holds the real meanings of the hymns—hymns otherwise fast becoming meaningless in the habitual repetition of abstract theological symbolism.

Not many of Bach's contemporaries are likely to have understood those delicate and subtle translations of religious thought; but perhaps a few believers and musically quickened persons may have been able to follow the commentary with which Bach surrounded and decorated the central themes. For us such pieces can only be enjoyed as mere music; can only be understood if we first connect up the associations of the music with the words, and then unravel the deeper and more material meanings which were hidden in the theological terminology.[2]

At Arnstadt Bach made two such pieces: the one

[1] Menzel, III, 20.
[2] See M. Widor's preface to Schweitzer's book; and in this connection Professor Sandon Terry deserves our gratitude for having provided English translations.

with the interesting pedal-part to which I have already alluded; the other, 'Wie schon leuchtet der Abend-stern,' of less poetic, but more musical virtue. Neither of these gives any indication of the development which he attained later on in this form. He was still experimenting, not only in the technical possibilities of his instrument, but also in the realistic limitations of music itself.

We have already studied the earliest indications of realistic tendency in Bach's music. Before the composer settled down to exploit the ground he had surveyed, he made one or two experiments to see if he could extend its boundaries. Among those experiments was a secular imitation of the form proposed by Kuhnau in his Bible Sonatas.

Kuhnau was a pioneer in musical realism. He made the inevitable mistakes of pioneers, but he stumbled upon interesting and important things. He concerned himself chiefly with physical things, so that his artistic expression seldom got beyond a childish plane. He chose historical incidents from the Old Testament, and occasionally they are not without emotional implications which nearly result in genuine expression. His music for the Israelites when they are confronted with Goliath conveys something of the idea of mob terror. His music for Saul in his madness has a mood which would have carried a musician with more emotional ease right over into the realm of creative art. But Kuhnau did not entirely reject the futility of musical materialism, as when David's pebble enters the giant's forehead.

There is a knife edge of artistic judgment between such an effort and the similar but not identical realism of Bach when he sends souls to heaven by means of high notes, and to hell by means of low ones. Bach's heaven and hell were like the Paradiso and Inferno of Dante, mental states where anybody might be at any moment of the earthly life, and therefore closely connected with those emotional states which find in music the most intense and unalloyed expression.

Kuhnau's Goliath was a one-and-only person, a mere historical or legendary figure, the life and death of whom in no way concerned Kuhnau or any other living Christian. By means of such physical realism there is no revelation of some inevitable thing which, until exposed by artistic faculty, has been closed to the general imagination. Moreover, old Kuhnau told his story at such length that his strands of musical theme are not strong enough to hold the tale together. However, he did so nearly bring off a good thing that we cannot be surprised when Bach with his own realistic bias tried a hand at similar music. But the greater composer took himself less seriously.

Bach's choice of subject was personal and immediate.

A brother of his was going to Sweden, and he made a piano piece for the occasion. So doing it is clear that he was aware of the essentially comic nature of music upon a physical plane.

When Goliath fell to earth Kuhnau was very solemn about it, even though the listener smiled. Bach counted on that smile and played up to it. His Caprice on the Departure of a Brother is full of jolly things which do not happen by accident. None of its sections are long; all of them are shapely.

The subject chosen seems at first thought even less promising than that of the Goliath Sonata. The family leave-taking has a narrower range of event and possible emotion; but the themes are directed less to a picture of the subject, more towards its emotional aspects. The sympathetic persuasion of friends, the warnings of un-expected and unpleasant occurrences, the regrets and the fears—all such show an appreciation of the dramatic possibilities of music as exact as that shown with greater labour and fuller means by Wagner a hundred years later.

Moreover, Bach triumphs in an important matter which Wagner truly attempted, but only succeeded in bringing off in his later works: I mean in combining the fragments of realistic theme into an adequate form for the exigencies of an art which, like architecture, fails in default of such combination.

Not to overload our study with analysis, consider only two sections of the Caprice.

In the first section the friends gather to dissuade the

brother from his journey. The feeling of the drama takes the following emotional line: "I really shouldn't go if I were you. You surely can't be meaning to leave us! O, but that's nonsense! What good can you do there? Here, John, he thinks that there are plenty at home without him. Tell him he's a donkey. Well, of all the obstinate fellows!" And while the feeling follows that line, rising from gentle dissuasion to annoyance, the music rises with architectural and decorative restraint.

So also in the final section, where the call of the coach-horn is mingled with scraps of folk-tune from the postilion in hearty bank-holiday style, both horn-call and riding rhythm are moulded according to the laws of pure musical art. So well is this part of the work done that Spitta felt safe in minimising the dramatic nature of the piece. Schweitzer, on the other hand, though generally bent on emphasizing Bach's dramatic nature, misses the drama of which this work, no less than the Passions and church-cantatas, is a part.

Why was Bach's brother going to Sweden just then? Why should his friends object to his going, describe the possibilities of the journey in terms of doubt and anger, and make so loud a lamentation that the composer felt obliged to use the chromatic formula of his most poignant moods? One authority is content to explain that the brother went to play the oboe in the Swedish guard 'in a spirit of hero-worship.' That is a mere detail of the drama. Let us consider what were the relations existing just then between Saxony and Sweden.

As the French power was the protagonist of Catholicism, so was the northern power that of Protestantism. The Swedes had lately been attacked by a group of powers which included the Saxon king who had turned Catholic that he might succeed to the throne of Poland. His Saxon subjects, and even his own queen, remained Protestant in spite of Luther's agreement that the faith of a prince should be the faith of his people. The Swedes gave Augustus of Saxony and his allies a good drubbing. Then, following the diplomatic line which would most naturally appeal to a king who left three hundred and sixty children to be provided for, Augustus tried to win the Swedish king by sending to him as ambassador a famous courtesan. Protestant Charles was proof against the woman as against the warriors. Catholic Augustus then fell back for support on half-pagan Russia. 'Charles seized the opportunity to march rapidly through Silesia into Saxony, where he was hailed as a defender of the Protestant faith with an enthusiasm scarcely inferior to that with which Gustavus Adolphus had formerly been welcomed.'[1]

This business was going on from 1700 to 1706. Bach's Caprice was written at Arnstadt in 1704.

So we see that a member of Bach's own family was

[1] Menzel, *History* cited, II, 510.

leaving home to take service with a Protestant king who had been victorious over the ruler of the country where Bach lived—over the father of the king to whom the master later on dedicated his B Minor Mass. We see also that it was the Protestant cause which was pleasing to the people of Saxony, and not the Saxon-Polish-Catholic cause.

Clearly then, even so late as the first years of the eighteenth century, the original international idea of Christendom, which had so nearly been Catholic in fact as well as in name, still lingered in the hearts of the people of whom the Bachs were a part. The later divisions caused by petty patriotisms had not yet supplanted the original conception of Christian Catholicism in the hearts of the common people of Saxony. Not so much wonder, then, that Bach ended his Caprice with a merry song and rollicking fugal gallop instead of with a song of regret for the loss of his brother.

Before the young and high-spirited musician left Arnstadt he had one more tussle with his employers. He was asked to explain how he came to be found in church 'with a stranger maiden.' He referred his interrogators to the parson. The following year he married his cousin, Maria Barbara Bach. But before that happened he had left Arnstadt almost as contemptuously as he had worked there, not even collecting the balance of his salary.

Chapter Five

FROM PIETY TO PRUDENCE

IETISM was ranged against orthodox Lutheranism wherever German people retained the tradition of practical Christianity. It was a futile protest in theological terms against the capture of the Christian organization by anti-Christians. It was a protest against the pretence of Protestantism, voicing popular feeling against the backsliding of the bourgeoisie. It was an effort to reform the Reformation after its original goal had been obscured, and its present purpose of helping the trading classes to keep the masses in subjection had become evident.

At Arnstadt Bach had found Protestantism a respectable and official thing. The whole atmosphere was antagonistic to pietism. The musician had therefore been obliged to express the truth of his faith as it were in secret; to give symbolic utterance to ideas which were deprecated in action, and even in a straightforward literary and plastic art.

At Mühlhausen, whither Bach went from Arnstadt, he had every reason to expect a different state of affairs. There was no petty prince there to exert an immediate influence upon the activities of the people. Mühlhausen was a 'free Imperial city'—somewhat of a contradiction in terms, but it meant that, being subject only to the Emperor at Vienna, mental freedom was more possible because of the distance between the people and their overlord. Though the Emperor was a Catholic it was not easy for him to exert over the city that degree of religious tyranny which he was entitled to employ under the bargain made between the Catholic and Lutheran officials at Augsburg.

The so-called freedom of such cities had already been revoked; but Mühlhausen was situated in a definitely Protestant part of the Empire, and had preserved certain links with the old civic spirit when the towns had been very nearly free in fact. How strongly entrenched was the popular will may be gathered from the fact that Frohne, the chief rector, was not even an orthodox Lutheran, but a Pietist! He was a much loved man of exemplary life.

At the very time of Bach's appointment reactionary influences were at work to displace the rector; but it is hard to believe that Bach was aware of them, at any rate before he had settled there.

That the musician should wish to be associated with such a city at such a time seems a further indication that his own mind was still in line with the tradition of his family. He had by no means been obliged to leave Arnstadt. In spite of his careless and rude attitude to

the church officials there, they had given no sign or
suggestion of dismissal. But the attitude of the ruling
class at Arnstadt was 'wholly unfavourable to pietism;'[1]
and, as we have seen, the Bach family tradition would
in these later times find in pietism their natural expression.

So far as we are aware of the working of John Sebastian's own mind in his art, he had steadily maintained
the tradition up to that time; no overt act of his suggested that he was moving away from it. Later on there
were two or three actions of a doubtful kind. There
was his increasing intimacy with Eilmar, a recreant parson who had apparently been brought to Mühlhausen
to undermine the position of the much-loved Frohne.
There was a more definite indication a few years later,
when Bach insisted that his children should receive a
rigidly orthodox education. But the weight of evidence
suggests that when the master first took up the appointment he was entirely in tune with the traditions of his
forbears.

What is of special importance for us, as we study this
vital moment in Bach's career, is to realise the frame of
mind in which he entered upon his new employment;
and then, so well as evidence permits, to trace the
gradual stiffening of his character as he came to grips
with the increasing difficulties of life.

In readiness to face realities Bach never failed; his

[1] Spitta, I, 364.

attitude to life was as realistic as his attitude to art. An example of that realism in life is to be seen in the very manner of the new appointment.

Before informing his Arnstadt masters that he was thinking of leaving their service, he seems to have entered into negotiations with the Mühlhausen Council—by no means anxiously, for they doubted whether they would be able to afford the terms he was expected to ask. Such caution—putting up with the pompous severity of the Arnstadt high-and-mighties until he was certain of a new post, and, notwithstanding his wish to make a change, giving the Mühlhausen burghers no hint of his anxiety—such business-like wariness proves the working of a mind by this time unwilling to take a single step without feeling confident of the issue.

This man is the child of the infant who had been robbed of the fruit of his midnight labour; of the boy who had known the necessity of choosing a music-school where he could earn money, though it were by singing in the streets; of the youth who had tasted domestic service in one of those houses of princely pretension, sensuality, and extravagance which made German courts a byword, until the house of Brandenburg whipped the others to heel; child also of the young man who had discovered that even in municipal service it is possible to suffer petty tyranny, not physically dangerous, but more exasperating in its fatuous incompetence than anything he was likely to have endured as personal servant of Prince George of Weimar.

After such early experiences is it probable that he would have transferred himself from orthodox Arnstadt, where he had plenty of time for his own work, to pietist Mühlhausen, with an immediate intention of getting married, but with no increase of salary; and, in spite of his acknowledged power as organist, have submitted himself to a competitive trial before a jury of his musical inferiors—unless he were expecting some greatly desired advantage? What could that advantage have been but a greater freedom to express the spirit that was within him?

Bach went to Mühlhausen knowing that the part of the city where his church stood was in ruins, having suffered seriously from fire a few months before his appointment. He knew that the general musical life there was in a backward state. It was better even in the villages of the neighbourhood!

Can we get some personal and living idea of the man as he faces these odds?

One of his portraits gives[1] something of the spirit which was moving within him at the time. It is a miniature in pencil and water-colour showing full cheek, heavy double chin, and fleshy nose, promising nothing of the punch-like form we see in a later and better-

---

[1] Reproduced in the *Musical Standard*, August 31, 1895, from an original then in the possession of Herr Edwin Bormann, of Leipsig.

known portrait. Such features might be those of a merchant well on the way to success; but in the open brow,
the mouth, and the eyes, there lives quite another
nature. The mouth has beauty without meanness; and
though it is ripe and merry, it could evidently close very
firmly. The eyes are full of light and laughter; but they
glitter with a fire that could freeze as well as kindle.
The brow is such as we expect to find in any well
developed human being.

Given normal conditions of development, that is the
sort of man who can add generously to the strength
and happiness of his kind; but such mouth, in association
with such chin and cheeks, indicates a large sensual
appetite which will not readily be deprived of life's
good material things. High faculties are there, fixed
in forehead and flowing from eyes; they will always see
life truly and judge it fairly. But will they be able to
take control when material conditions become difficult?
The nose is tenacious, but in no way indicative of an
adventurous nature. In that face the will to hold is
more apparent than the will to explore. Such a man will
maintain the highest that he knows; but whether he
will be able to seek out still higher things in spite of
difficulty and hardship is another matter, and it is ex-
tremely unlikely that he will knowingly take any road
which would involve him in serious embarrassment.

A man of that kind would surely have avoided
Mühlhausen in 1707 if he had been definitely anti-

pietist. That, I think, is beyond doubt, for it is unlikely that he had no idea of local conditions before accepting the appointment.

There is certainly a possible alternative, though of an unpleasant kind.

It would seem as if Eilmar had been introduced to the city by those who were intent on ousting Frohne on account of his popular and pietist tendencies. There is no documentary evidence of that idea, so far as I am aware; but no one who studies the situation, and knows how such people go to work, can doubt that something of that kind happened; for directly Eilmar was appointed and began to attack Frohne the new man had definite support from the municipal authorities.[1]

Pietism placed a definite bar on certain developments of art, and as we already know, however nearly in agreement Bach may have been with the rational and real religion, he did not, could not, agree that the imagination which moved within him was other than a power for good.

Now if Eilmar was expected to help in undermining the independent spirit of the people it is possible that Bach may have been engaged by the same scheming group, with the idea of joining the seductive beauty of music to the less attractive influences of official opinion and dogma. The fact that Bach himself was of pietist tendency would be no bar to such use of him. On the

[1] Spitta, I, 359-60.

contrary, it is well known to all students of history that such authorities, when they are not quite sure of the forces at their disposal, prefer to use men whose record would tend to lull the suspicions of the general public.

Eilmar was not the pastor of Bach's own church; yet he seems to have laid himself out to be agreeable to his hated colleague's organist: for example, by writing cantata-librettos. Bach would certainly respond very warmly to an advance of that kind—the more so because his own pastor, beloved and finer spirited though he was, had yet the oppressive limitations of those who hesitate to approve good things because bad people enjoy them.

Knowledge of the characters of those two clergymen, however, could scarcely have been clear in Bach's mind when he entered upon the engagement; and if his art had really been required for the subversion of popular religion the organist would probably have been the last to learn the fact. It seems almost certain that he expected to find in the 'free city' freedom for his art, and for the sort of expression which had been hindered by the anti-pietist authorities of Arnstadt. Judging by the relations which developed during his life at Mühlhausen, he was not entirely disappointed.

So when, in the autumn of 1707, Bach took a wagonload of musical instruments and other possessions from the one place to the other, we may believe that his heart was full of the natural generosity of early manhood, even though tempered by the caution which earlier hardships had implanted in him. He was in love. He had the exhilarating sense of growing artistry. He was just free from the restraints of a place where respectable Lutheranism had held soul, and even body, in thrall; where young Treiber had had to choose between an emasculated mind and a starved body; where he had been expected to teach a lot of tiresome boys their notes, even to the detriment of his own creative faculty. He was now to be an important public servant in a city where the general will of the people exerted some degree of influence in public affairs; where the essential principles of Christian doctrine were being disseminated by his own parson; where real religion was allowed the fullest measure of expression in those reactionary times. And in spite of the dilemma with which he was soon faced, the master's life at Mühlhausen seems to have fulfilled some at least of his expectations, more especially the personal ones.

He immediately began to develop the musical life of the place. His external activities showed a larger element of initiative than before or after that time.

At Arnstadt his greater powers were certainly unappreciated; he experienced there a certain amount of obstruction which must have caused in him real mental depression—not in the sense of a mood of melancholy, but in the more literal and vital sense of the word—

because of the dead pretences which weighed upon his efforts to give musical expression to the realities of life.

At Mühlhausen that weight seems to have been lifted, and he contributed to the musical life of the place, not merely as a paid official, but for love of the work itself. That is the more noteworthy because, as Professor Terry acutely points out, Bach always objected to being saddled with any work which was not stated in the contract of his engagement.

For example, the musical library of the church of St. Blasius had been destroyed in the big fire; and though it was the duty of another musician to provide the music, Bach enlarged the new library at his own expense. Furthermore, he seems to have been in genial relation with the pietist congregation, as a whole, quite apart from his official connections. The parishioners were anxious to have a set of bells attached to the new organ, and were themselves willing to find the money for it. Such communal enthusiasm must have seemed very pleasant to the organist after his experience of Mr. Stomach, the tomb-bargaining organ-giver of Arnstadt; and a carillon was accordingly included in the specification which Bach drew up. It appears that the bells were not finally incorporated; but that, I imagine, was due to no lack of will on the part of Bach, whose love of bells is proved by many a page of his music. The congregational pleasure was probably overborne in this detail, as eventually in the more vital matter of pietism.

To begin with, there was a more immediate relation between the organist and the people he was engaged to serve. It was no mere personal accident, but a part of the general spirit of a city where medieval traditions of communal Christianity still lingered in political form as well as in some external customs.

The church itself bore witness in stained glass, beaten iron, and carven stall, to the living faith which had once been translated into art as well as into action. Though Bach's appointment may or may not have originated in the partisans of Eilmar and of orthodoxy, the form on an election persisted. Another reminder of the ways of the Middle Ages was the manner of the organist's pay; it included 'three measures of corn, two trusses of wood, one of beech, one of oak or aspen, six trusses of faggots, delivered at his door in lieu of arable.' There we have a link with the time when the organist took his share in the communal ownership of the land, and followed his turn at the plough.

Most important evidence of all for the purpose of our present study was a cantata he made for a civic ceremony. This is now known as the Rathswahl or Rathwechsel Cantata—for the election, or the changing, of the city council—and the alternative title is significant.

Mühlhausen was governed by a council consisting

of forty-eight burghers, of whom six were entitled to the position of mayor. One third of these carried on the executive work in rotation, so that (as one authority notes) the ceremony cannot be regarded as pertaining to an election, but rather to a change of councillors. A proclamation regarding the change was read from the pulpit on the Sunday preceding, and called for the 'election' of a new council. But that was eyewash. The terminology of an older and freer time had been retained, but evidently the people no longer possessed the real power of choice. The parts of Bach's cantata printed under his supervision are more frank and refer to the 'change' of council. I am not splitting hairs in the matter of the title. That kind of alteration, whereby the people were deprived of the reality of power even while its pretence was emphasised, has always been one of the more subtle means whereby self-seekers have managed to hold the reins of government. The cantata itself contains evidence of the human suffering and resentment which formed the background of the change, and more than a hint of Bach's ideas regarding the rights and wrongs of the case.

The first significant number is the duet which was intended to express the dramatic idea of a change of servants. Bach indicates no mere change from respectable burgher to respectable burgher. The voices chosen are tenor and soprano, man and boy. The expression of outworn service is given to the adult, and the words are of one whose work is completely over rather than of a burgher who will again be on the executive in three years' time. For Bach the hope of the future was in the next generation, and the boy sang words expressing that hope.

Still more significant, is the fact that, while the music for the departing servant suggests ineffectual labour, the music expressing hope for the future is—not an expression of Bach's personal mind suggesting joy and security instead of failure and defeat, though it is clear that he could easily have made such a music— but one of the peoples' own songs, a chorale.

Having these historical clues, we see that no music could more fitly express the failure and wrong of the accepted methods of government than that which Bach has associated with the councillor who makes his exit, even as the popular song in the mouth of the boy indicates that the hope for the future lay with the youth of the people themselves.

Another piece which is specially revealing of the composer's mind is the aria, 'Through mighty power.' It is one of those pretentious military thanksgivings by means of which various nations take in vain the names of their gods for their victories over one another.

> On our side didst Thou fight
> With power and great might!

Bach sets it for trumpets and drums to a music which would stir no deep feeling in any heart. It expresses the blatant safe-at-home valour of fat burghers who felt specially petted by the Most High—and by his slaves below, the thoughtless soldiery of the Emperor. Those last, however, were luckily fighting elsewhere at that time. They were preferred at a distance, however holy their cause!

The real thoughts and feelings which flooded Bach's mind as a result of the association of bloody war and divine power wrung from him the truer music of the next number—most deeply significant in the whole cantata. It is a chorus to the words, 'O deliver not the soul of thy turtle-dove unto the multitude of the wicked.'

A composer concerned only with aesthetic fitness would certainly have regarded such words as more suitable for solo-setting. Bach allotted them to the chorus which most definitely expressed the emotions of the people as a body. The music is dark and poignant.

The composer knew that from the earliest period of the Christian era unto his own day the bodies and minds of gentle and harmless working people had regularly been delivered into the hands of those who cared chiefly for material wealth and political power. This is not a book of martyrs, but as a study of Bach's significance in the history of Christian art it will fail of its effect if we do not bear in mind certain historic details which are too often forgotten when the subject-matter is concerned with the beauties of art.

Passing by the earliest periods of Christian martyrdom, and the middle period of Christian joy when the
peoples of Western Europe seemed as if they really
meant to build the Kingdom of Heaven on earth, let us
recall a few incidents the steady decline of Christendom
from the Middle Ages to Bach's own day.

In 1204 was the Albigensian crusade, when the Pope,
the chief official of the international body of Christians,
'offered the feudal lords of Central and Northern
France the same remission of sins as for Crusaders in
the East' if they would do bloody work among a simple
people whose chief crime was their denunciation of
'worldly bishops and robber barons.'[1]

In 1380 there had been the ruthless suppression of
the Florentine workers who had gained complete control of their republic, and in their executive existence
of three years showed 'unsuspected qualities of wisdom
and restraint.'[2]

There had been the burning of Huss in Bohemia in
1415 and the foul class-wars which followed; in 1498
the execution of Savonarola at the instigation of Alexander VI, the poisoner Pope, whose infamies gave the
cue to all the blackguard priests and kings of the Renaissance.[3]

There had been the so-called Peasants' War which

[1] Thorndike, *Medieval Europe*, pp. 421-4.
[2] Sismondi, *History of the Italian Republics*, Book V.
[3] Machiavelli's *Life and Times*, Eng. transl. by Villari, pp. 268,
282, 285, 306-9.

had had its headquarters in Bach's own country of Thuringia, and was really a struggle by the masses of German folk to bring about the organization of life according to Christian principles.[1] And it is especially interesting for us to remember that Mühlhausen had been the people's stronghold in that war. The memory of the people is a long memory, and the tradition of freedom so nearly won would not be without its influence even in Bach's time—the more so because acts of bloodshed and beastliness were not yet past. Bach was indeed able to sing in his civic cantata,

> Our peace by none's disturbed,
> Though war's alarms and strife
> Around us rage and swell;

but no one knew how long it would be before the old devilments recurred.

As recently as 1631 Magdeburg had been "stormed, plundered, and almost destroyed, amid scenes of horror which made the event noticeable in an age of lust and cruelty."[2]

Of course, these were but tales and memories in Bach's day, and the suggestion was probably made that 'our days are not as the days of our fathers'; but as a matter of fact, the evil thing was still going on. We have already seen how Bach's brother declared for

[1] Engels, *Peasant War in Germany.*
[2] A. W. Holland's *Germany* (Making of Nations Series), p. 185.

the popular cause. Here is another bit of history of close interest:

'The restoration of Augustus to the throne by Russia had greatly embittered the Poles, and the Saxons fell frequent victims to assassination. Augustus in revenge sought to curb the spirit of the people by the most violent measures, and placed them totally under the control of the Jesuits. In 1724 the citizens of Thorn being compelled to bend the knee during a passing procession of Jesuits, by whom some innocent persons were treated with horrible cruelty, the populace revolted, rescued one of the prisoners, and destroyed part of the Jesuit college. The burgomaster Roesner, together with eight of the citizens, were in revenge sentenced to the block by a criminal court established for that purpose by the king. The executioner, tearing the heart from the palpitating bosom of one of the victims, exclaimed, "Behold, a Lutheran's heart! " " [1]

The Augustus referred to in the above quotation was the father of the King of Poland and Elector of Saxony, to whom Bach subsequently dedicated the B minor Mass! However, at the Mühlhausen stage of the composer's development he had certainly not reached the point where that sort of dedication was possible. We have already seen him openly serving the Protestant

---

[1] Menzel, *Hist. of Germany*, Eng. transl., II, 517. For a more intimate idea of the time than it is possible to give here the reader may be referred to Feuchtwanger's famous novel, *Jew Süss*.

cause, and musically serving the Pietists, the most earnest section of the Protestants.

But he knew that not only Catholic officials, but Protestant officials also, had delivered the minds of Christians to suffering and stupidity as their bodies to torture and death. He knew that at Arnstadt young Treiber had not been allowed to live according to his own principles, or even to declare them openly, but had been obliged to lie in order to earn his bread. He knew that the great black cloud from Rome had been dispersed in places only to be followed by the frosts and hails of bourgeois Lutheran formalism.

How could the composer pray for deliverance 'calmly and trustfully' when Arnstadt was only a few miles distant?

Even in the 'free city' of Mühlhausen the people were no longer free to elect their own government, but must content themselves with proclamations which oiled them with specious words of freedom and 'evangelical Christianity,' reproving all 'greed and self-seeking,' while in fact they continued to be governed by just such burghers as made the town safe for greedy and self-seeking men.

Pietism certainly made a good stand there. For seventeen years Dean Frohne had stood fast by the popular cause in the narrow theological sphere which was all that remained of highest life for enslaved and revolting spirits; and the persistence of even the theory of freedom in words of obscure symbolism was worth something. It stirred people with a vague sense of their lost and vanishing rights, and did something to ward off further aggression in the way, for instance, that Christian theory was not without influence in modifying factory conditions in England a hundred years later.

Year by year, we are told, 'pietism gained a broader foothold among the German people.'[1] That does not merely mean that the uneducated German masses preferred one sort of subtle religious theory to another sort. It means that the theory was, in their minds, an expression of material need and hope.

When first the pietist movement started, its full implications were not realised by orthodox Lutherans, and there was little or no opposition to it. It was only when the theory was 'carried out vigorously in practice that the opposition began.' However, the bourgeoisie had already learned the unwisdom of direct attack; it made things too uncomfortable for themselves. But what cannot be easily overthrown by frontal attack may often be spoiled by flanking movement or strategem, if men are willing and can afford to wait, and especially if the position to be taken is held only by simple, honest, and gentle people.

So, nine years before Bach's move to Mühlhausen, Archdeacon Eilmar had been brought into the place; and, in his attack upon the principles preached by

[1] Spitta's *Bach*, I, 358.

Frohne, the newcomer was openly approved by some of the municipal authorities. Eilmar advocated in theologese what the Duke of Weimar said more bluntly a little later on. The aristocratic enemy of the people said that they 'were not to reason under pain of correction.' The traitor parson said that it was 'heretical to pray for special enlightenment when reading the scriptures.' As Spitta remarks, 'this was certainly the standpoint of orthodoxy to which they [the Lutherans] had been driven to subscribe by the struggle. The first principle of Lutheranism was already lost to them; the church was to them almost as to the Catholics, something perfect and divine, whose means of grace her children need only receive passively, and whose ministers considered themselves as the bearers of a divine official gift which was perfectly independent of their moral conduct; while pietism, on the contrary, strove to develop afresh the fundamental idea of Protestantism.'[1]

It is a perennial story, and we still have it with us. Organizations are slowly developed by the people with a view to their own welfare; but the officials engaged to administer them grow to regard themselves as a superior folk, and the organizations as existing for their own peculiar benefit. From that moment control of such organizations is very easily acquired by the very tyranny against which they were formed.

At Mühlhausen the enemies of the people did not

[a] Spitta, I, 259.

quite so easily undermine the reformed church. Popular feeling was too strongly in favour of Frohne for Eilmar to gain a quick victory. The open dispute between the elderly dean and the young archdeacon was referred, not to an ecclesiastical authority, but to the town council. That in itself bears witness to a strong tradition of popular government, and showed that the representatives of the people were regarded as sovereign, even though the dispute was wrapped up in theological phraseology. But the council no longer consisted of men who were chosen for their love of 'justice and righteousness,' their hatred of 'greed and self-seeking.' So Eilmar got no positive reproof, even though the attitude of the public was so definitely declared that the reactionaries dared not blame Frohne. There ensued the humbug of a 'moderate order.' Both parties were to 'refrain from controversy.' Thus it was suggested that in some obscure way Frohne was at least as culpable as his adversary.

Of course the trouble broke out again. All such troubles do. Eilmar was there chiefly to keep them alive. But the burghers had to wait for Frohne's death, when they proceeded at once to put the other man in his place. That, however, was later, after Bach had disappeared from the scene.

For the musician the dispute was probably the parting of the ways. His creative power, and therefore his inmost feelings, were with the pietists. His means of

livelihood, like young Treiber's, was at the disposal
of those who were opposed to everything the pietists
stood for. Once we understand that fact we can see
why Spitta and others have so often failed in a proper
interpretation of the master's works, even when correct
in their estimate of his aesthetic values. Thus, though
the biographer could not understand why Bach's Rathwechsel Cantata took on such original emotional expressions, he did most wonderfully gauge its artistic
tendency: he felt the nature of the prayer for deliverance 'from the multitude of the wicked,' even though he
did not see how Bach himself was encompassed by that
very multitude. He regarded the music as a 'failure of
the highest psychological interest' because he was almost
entirely concerned with Bach's personal psychology as
artist, and omitted to consider the greater psychological forces which affect even the greatest artists. May it
not be, indeed, that the greatest artists owe their extra
power, not only to their greater industry and skill as
craftsmen, but also to an increased susceptibility to the
mass-psychology of their time?

So, when Bach's biographer instinctively connected
that choral prayer for deliverance with the deepest utterances of the master—the music of the *Crucifixus* in
the B minor Mass—and at the same time declared it to
be a failure of the highest psychological interest, his
puzzlement arose because he did not understand how
the Crucifixion was something more than an historical

fact or a mystical symbol—that it was indeed a recurrent reality for all the truest Christians from the thirteenth century onwards.

Bach as an artist did exactly what the masses of Christendom had done—he typified the gentle man who was willing to suffer for the general welfare and for truth.

His music reveals where his inmost sympathies were in that particular dispute. Now let us try to understand how he came to be in dispute with the leader of the pietists.

Already, it appears, he had had trouble regarding the music at Frohne's own church of St Blasius. We know that Bach's genius sought an enlargement and extension of religious feeling in flights beyond the average understanding. That music had for its objective the goal towards which Frohne was striving along another channel; but the parson, drily ethical perhaps, was unable to see it.

We have learned how, during the decay of vocal polyphony, the organ was introduced into churches to buttress up the failing musical structure; how in time it became a mechanical device, serving at first to hide the fact that the people were no longer singing for the joy they had in the diversity of Christian unity; and finally how the instrument usurped the place of the popular singing, making automatic antiphony to the official sentences of the priest.

In the high tide of Protestant revolt the people once again took possession of the musical parts of the church service, employing their own folk songs with such religious words as seemed to declare the reality of Christianity. Thus many German folk-songs had become hymn-tunes; and Bach, like other organists of Protestant faith, used the instrument for the purpose of giving to those songs the practical support of accompaniment and sensual warmth of harmony. A proportion of the congregation, with that instinctive harmonic sense which seems to be possessed by a few in any singing crowd, probably followed the bass and groped about for middle parts. They may not have been capable of much more than that; but at the same time they would be no more willing to hand over all their function as singers to the musical officials than the other communal elements of worship to the clerical officials. But that was not the whole of the difficulty, or a solution of the problem for Frohne and Bach might have been possible.

Bach's training and integrity as a musician were bound up with an elaborate technic, while the pietists were simple people to whom such technic was almost a foreign tongue, and sounded like meaningless display; but in this matter I think Bach had the deeper truth on his side.

The original polyphony of the Catholic Church had been no mere device of musical craftsmanship, but the natural expression of an intelligent and cultured community wherein every member was alive in separateness, necessarily obliged to preserve the order which gave unity to the mingled parts, and sharing in the increase of joy and richness which so many well disciplined individualities contributed to the whole. In that way the music reflected the finest political ideas of the old communes.

Bach himself was the culmination of a prolonged effort made by professional musicians to develop a like means of expression in the service of the reformed church. But there were at least two important differences between the old and the new polyphony. Catholic polyphony had been grafted upon the people's own songs and was essentially vocal. By the time that Protestantism had become sufficient of a power to require its own music, economic conditions had caused the arts to be developed in the interests of the bourgeoisie. The popular origin and associations of the arts were less evident. Musical polyphony had passed from the simpler vocal stage into more elaborate and difficult instrumental forms.

Even so, every notable development of Bach's creative genius was in the nature of a step towards the people—not to the people as they were, alas! but to the people as they would have been if their musical opportunities had been equal to their masonic opportunities in the thirteenth century. That natural tendency of Bach towards the popular need and understanding crops up continually throughout his career. It shows itself even in so unexpected a direction as his specifications and proposals for the improvement of organs. He wished to make the instrument less of a dominating factor in the religious service, more of a communal convenience and support.[1] Other details of that same tendency are the master's passion for the people's own tunes, and his treatment of solo instruments, not only in the concertos, but in association with arias. These are matters which we shall consider in some detail later on. Here only to recognize the general tendency of his art as an expression of the minds of free folk in communal relationship. It may be that his efforts were instinctive rather than conscious; but it is none the less obvious to the student of musical history, and its very unconsciousness would make it in some ways the more significant.

However, to have effected a real and fruitful relationship with simple people of strong faith but undeveloped aesthetic capacity was practically impossible. For that it would have been necessary that the artist should have been aware of historical and political problems beyond the ability of man then to gather together; necessary also that he should renounce a great part of his own skill as musical craftsman, and any musician who has tried to do that will know that there is no harder task.

To Frohne and most of his pietist congregation Bach

[1] Terry's *Bach*, p. 81.

may have seemed a stubborn maker of music who thought more of his own doings than of the simple and straightforward worship of God. To Bach the matter probably seemed more of a dispute between an ignorant and sometimes fanatical majority, and a cultured and sympathetic minority, the majority intent only on the most obvious forms of religious worship, the minority capable of appreciating those subtle moods of mysticism for which music is the perfect medium. The minority may have seemed a little careless of the more definite ideas which informed the composer's religious music; but, on the other hand, the greater sympathy which they with their wider culture offered to the man, must have counted for a good deal, and might even have caused him to feel that they were not so far from his own religious position, though they were more orthodox in outward show.

As for the musical ideas of the pietists in relation to Bach they were most likely completely Philistine. The exuberances of Bach upon the organ were for himself manifestations of divine impulse: the industry and skill which enabled him to use his material with freedom were proofs that his will was to give the very best service in his power, while the polyphonic forms he used vouched for the perfect equality of all voices and parts in that service. But to many of the pietists Bach's exuberances will have seemed proud vauntings of personal agility and showmanship, and the very forms which were intended to express Christian equality will have sounded like the pretentious pedantry of the superior person. To the bourgeois church-goers, on the other hand, their organist's skill must have seemed very satisfactory evidence of the wisdom of their investment; it proved the excellence of their artistic judgment, while the sounds he made in their more leisured and cultured ears were as spiritual oils working upon a good mental digestion and leathern conscience.

Not even the most devoted admirer of Bach's art can fail to sympathise with people who want to sing their songs straight through, without having to wait between each line for an organ flourish, or between each verse for an organ interlude—threads and tapestries of music beyond the understanding of hard-worked people. Not even the most skilled contrapuntist will fail to understand that a simple and primitive musical taste must absorb the full joy of a single melodic line before it can begin to find pleasure in a web of polyphony.

We must also remember that the recurring opposition between artists and puritans is almost entirely due to an evil economic relationship which leads most artists to accept service with people who can afford to pay them well, people who are likely to associate their artistic pleasures with other less healthy luxuries. There inevitably arises in the minds of poorer men a feeling of contempt for artists who, however unwillingly, are functioning as parasites; and a feeling of resentment however unintentional, because poverty is depriving them of an important educational right.

Furthermore, artists working in a parasitical relationship are bound to produce works, not only limited in the range of their appeal, but limited in their aesthetic value. It seems hard to believe that in the case of Bach. It seems hard for any living musician to believe that a nobler music could exist; but it is not unreasonable to think that if the psychological atmosphere of Bach's time had been less heavy with the dull thunder of the people's suppressed anger, the master's own spirit would have been proportionately invigorated.

As it was he was expressing ideas akin to those of the stunted majority of the poorest. Such an artist is in the unfortunate position of a workman whose only possible employers have an idea of life which depends on the continuance of bad conditions—of a workman whose work is not wanted by those who would, if they were decently educated, most appreciate it and benefit from it.

Beethoven in that position took his employer's money and called him an ass. Bach made a fight, but finally did what Wagner and others have done in a like case— took service with the enemy.

We have now reached the moment in his career when he made that change, withdrawing from a public service which had become impossible except for men of quixotic or despicable kind. The master decided to take private service where, if he could not express the deepest feelings of his time for men who in any case were unable to make use of his work, he could at least preserve his own integrity as artist, and perhaps cherish a secret flame—the flame which had burned so brightly in the days when Protestantism blazed up against the betrayal of Catholicism, or even the steadier flame which had lighted all Western Europe when Catholic meant, not Roman and official, but international and popular.

Bach did succeed in cherishing that flame to the end of his days. What Spitta calls a 'predilection for dark and deeply moved conditions of the soul' was not a personal thing at all. It was due to the sultry mental atmosphere of the time. It was an inevitable expression wrung from the artist against the tendency of his own naturally exultant nature.

Wolf, the song-writer, said that 'the true test of greatness in a composer is, Can he exult?' But it is equally a test of greatness in the sense of largeheartedness (and unless the word carries that significance in relation to art it is valueless) that a composer be true to the reality of his life and time. So, in the words of his biographer, 'the fear of possible danger became deepened with him' in the choral prayer for deliverance from the Rathwechsel cantata, 'into the agony of a mind tormented to the last degree by terror and distress.'

Since popular Christianity failed, that agony, equally with a capacity for joy, has been a part of the mentality of every artist who has been deeply sensitive of feeling and fearless of intellectual realism. Those artists whose sensitiveness outweighed their capacity for imaginative joy—Botticelli and Dowland, for examples—subsided into melancholy and silence. Those artists whose personal virility maintained a healthier emotional balance —Dante, Bach, Blake, Beethoven—found symbolical ways of suggesting the realities which most men feared or denied.

Had Bach been incapable of such intellectual realism, or had he failed to find adequate symbolic forms for its expression, he would have been of no greater distinction than his son, Philip Emanuel. The son's ability to adapt himself to Renaissance culture proved to be readier than the father's; but the very ability so to adapt himself was proof of a less sensitive mind, a more superficial attitude to the deepest things of life. It was John Sebastian's will to look facts in the face, probe them to the core, and then find some means of expressing them from skin to spirit, even though they carried implications which were lost, or ignored, or hated, by the majority of cultured people—it was such a combination which made him the greatest artist of his own evil day, and perhaps the greatest artist who ever lived. It is also that same combination which made his general behaviour in life rational, though to the pietists he may have seemed a traitor, and to the orthodox a fanatical old fool.

Considering how he maintained his inner veracity to the end of his life, considering his moderate capacity for work involving discreet drudgery, and considering his domestic responsibilities, few will doubt that his line of action was right. He derived little material benefit and less renown than many who were vastly inferior to him; and in the double intellectual life which he pursued to the end of his days he can have found little understanding or friendship—probably only that of his second wife. He had a certain range of social acquaintance including Eilmar himself, but no friend with whom he could discuss in open words the closed thoughts he was for ever hinting in his music.

His cantata for the change of council had relation to the dispute which was rending the whole community of Mühlhausen. None of them understood that. Those who praised it for its artistic qualities did not know that its spirit and intention were popular and pietist. It was written in the interests of men who were not sufficiently mentally developed to enjoy it, who regarded it with indifference, as an artist's conceit, or even as a work of the devil.

So he resigned his position.

However, the manner of his resignation was not as from Arnstadt. There, where pietism was hated and orthodox Lutheranism supreme, he had treated his employers with contempt. At Mühlhausen, where Frohne remained in control, supported by the love of the pietist masses of the people, the musician resigned with expressions of gentle goodwill and even regret. He contented himself with pointing out that certain musical difficulties had arisen which proved to be impossible of adjustment. Even after his departure he continued to be responsible for the restoration of the organ he had planned.

And so he went to Weimar to take menial service with a Grand Duke.

Chapter Six

GOTHIC V. RENAISSANCE IN MUSIC

BACH was now out of the fray for a time. Such an engagement as he had taken with the Grand Duke of Weimar was generally associated with personal and domestic service. There are several instances of such association in the records of the Bach family. One member of the family had been engaged as 'artist and musician' at the Abbey of Gandersheim, an institution where the arts had been fostered during the dark ages, as witness the plays of Roswitha the nun. In the agreement concerning that appointment Nicholas Ephraim Bach was named as a 'lackey.' His annual wage was to be twenty dollars, with two liveries, travelling coats and stockings, and a weekly allowance of twenty groats for food. Later on he was promoted to be cup-bearer and then butler, in which final condition of eminence he was set over the abbey servants, and took charge of their artistic and musical education.

Another Bach had been 'court-lackey and oboe-player.' Yet another, very near to Sebastian in point of time, was so evidently in bondage that his employer was able to refuse him leave of absence that he might visit his children who lived at a distance, even though he offered to leave a deputy in charge of the organ.

Such had been the conditions of musico-domestic service for the earlier generations of Bachs; and it is clear that the conditions were still of some indignity in the time of the greatest member of the family. In Weimar the burgomaster 'himself served the Duke in the menial office once filled by Bach's grandfather.'

Some of the composer's biographers try to ease our thoughts of his position by praising his employer; but it is hard to harmonise the circumstances of Bach's life there with such praise.

The Duke was something of a religious fanatic even in his orthodoxy. One of the things recorded in his honour is a sermon which he preached at the age of eight; another, the assiduity he showed in arranging special religious training for the 'lower classes.' But he would not allow his subjects to meet together for their own religious worship; and when appointing a preacher he made sure that the man would expect no freedom of expression. The Duke demanded a Lutheran uniformity as uncompromising as that of the most rigid Roman authority. He required 'universal assent to the dogmatic proposition that the gifts of even unconverted ministers were saving and effectual by virtue of their office.' He caused points of religious difference to be narrowly investigated by the scholars of Jena (the uni-

versity whence young Treiber had been expelled because he demanded the right to think freely); after such
investigation the Duke announced 'in a full and particular rescript how he would have them decided.'[1]

Of course, all this religious care and severity had for
its ultimate object the political and economic control of
the people who lived in the duchy. Members of the
duke's own class were allowed plenty of latitude. He
himself had in his time kept a court-fool and held hunts
and carnivals, although such festivities involved incon-
venience and even suffering for the peasants and workers. Moreover, he maintained the closest relation with
'the pleasure-loving court of Weissenfels'; and the
pleasures of the German courts in those days were not
exactly in the nature of puritan picnics.[2]

Even in Bach's time the duke enjoyed occasions of
extravagant and luxurious display. The composer made
his first secular cantata for a festival when 'the guests
sat down to a banquet at tables set amid exotic shrubs,
cypress, orange, almond, and myrtle, whose fragrance
turned a winter's evening to summer.'[3]

Of the Duke's appearance we are told that he had a
sharply cut and meagre face with a retreating forehead,
a large prominent nose and a somewhat projecting chin.

Into the service of that petty tyrant Bach entered,
and held a subordinate position as player upon clavier,

[1] Spitta, I, 377.
[2] Menzel, III, 17 onwards.
[3] Terry, *Bach*, p. 108.

organ, or fiddle, as might be required, under Drese the capellmeister. The livery he wore was that of a Hei-duck, a costume not unlike that donned by the so-called Hungarian bands favoured in London society during later Victorian times.

Despite all the Duke might dictate, however, there was evidently a truly religious life in the town of Wei-mar itself.

At the ducal court Italian music was in vogue. At the town church the organist, Walther, was noted for his adherence to the peoples' own songs. We are told that between Walther and Bach there was at first friend-ship and later division. It is easy to understand how two such men would be drawn together, and not hard to imagine how divergence might follow.

Walther was in a position of comparative artistic freedom, and could continue to develop such power as he had in a truly original way. Bach was obliged to study the pleasures of his master, and for a time, any-how, make the best case he could for the fashionable style of foreign music. The greater musician must have found it hard to maintain his integrity and excuse his footmanship.

However, having taken the service, Bach turned it as far as possible to his own advantage. A certain amount of heartless decorative music he was obliged to make, as performer if not as composer; but there were ways of serving the great power within him, even at that court. He could develop his skill as an executive artist, and compose special music for his own instruments.

The pieces he arranged and composed during the first years at Weimar are comparatively unimportant; but the pains he then took with all matters relating to the organ affected the whole of his subsequent career. The course pursued by him in regard to the organ indicates a possible cause for the weakening of artistic sympathy between him and Walther.

The chorale was the root and flower of Walther's musical conceptions; and the most noticeable thing in the music written by Bach during his years at Weimar is his neglect of the chorale. The people's songs, which had been the centre of his first musical thoughts, seem almost to have disappeared from his world. That is the more remarkable because of their original importance in the growth of organ music.

Schweitzer tells us that 'the chorale was the teacher of the organists, leading them from the false and fruitless virtuosity of the keyboard to the true simple organ style. . . . It is an illustration of how an idea is in the end stronger than circumstances. Organ music did not come to perfection in Paris or in Venice, where everything seemed to be in its favour, but among the poor cantors and schoolmasters of an impoverished country.'

Popular song has always been the tap-root of musical growth. There is a certain idiomatic strength in the people's own songs which seems to give to composers more than personal powers of expression. In Germany, where the folk-song tradition was most steadily maintained by professional musicians, the best music was made. In Elizabethan England and Russia under the last Czars, where there were cultural gaps between the common people and the professional musicians, the latter were forced to borrow from the former a proper basis for their work.[1]

We have examined one of Bach's earliest attempts to decorate the popular song. Such an experiment stands to his later works as primitive Celto-Saxon decoration to the finest expressions of Gothic. Beginning partly in a decorative instinct Bach, like the Gothic sculptors, realised that with increased skill he could pass from decoration to real expression. The detail, as he developed it, was sometimes subtly connected, sometimes diffuse, but on the whole it tended to be more and more realistic. Masons and musicians revealed more and more vividly in their decorative schemes ideas which expressed details of the main purpose of the buildings and the songs.

When the sculptors of the Renaissance passed from the service of the communes to the service of tyrants,

---

[1] See the folk-song arrangements in the Fitzwilliam Virginals Book, and the music of Glinka, Borodin, Rimsky Korsakoff, and other modern Russians. Even the plunging anarch, Stravinsky, fumbles for the same source of life, while for lack of it the works of Striabine stretch out palely like hot-house growths.

they passed from the service of life to the service of death—from the decoration of common houses of joy to the decoration of tombs from a vampire-hearted class. The so-called Rebirth was devoted chiefly to the service of Death. That is a matter of simple historic fact. With the end of the great period of cathedral building there was also an end of vulgar beauty and common incident in expressive sculptural detail.

Later on a similar breakdown occurred in the art of music. With the depreciation of Gothic polyphony in favour of Italian monody there was a temporary end of the folk-basis for musical art. The passage from cathedral building to coffin decoration has its exact parallel in the passage from happy music to sad music discussed in a previous chapter. The change is well expressed by the difference of feeling between the finest piece of thirteenth century music that we know—'Sumer is icumen in'—and Bach's despairing cry in the Rathwechsel cantata.

Becoming one of the Duke of Weimar's menials, Bach entered an atmosphere opposed to everything that had been expressed by the German chorale. Decadent art there reigned supreme. The duke's own palace was an example. Renaissance architecture offered a suitably dull exterior setting for the comparatively trivial musical thoughts of Corelli and Vivaldi. While, as Professor Terry remarks, 'not one of the sanctuaries Bach served matched so ill with his art' as the garish baroque and bizarre chapel of the duke.[1]

However much of economic relief the new engagement may have meant for Bach and his young wife, however much in the way of artistic opportunity he may have hoped for, the change cannot have been other than unpleasing to the artist who had recently been playing the music of the north German composers within the living walls of St. Blasius at Mühlhausen. Bach cannot have taken kindly to the foreign and superficial atmosphere. Though he ignored the chorale his early organ works of the Weimar period have less in common with the music of the Italian composers and more with his own native school.

At the same time he did his best. He made transcriptions of some Italian concertos. A comparison between them and his own original compositions of the Weimar period will be of interest, for the vital problem before Bach at that moment was whether he should become an original composer, or a court-confectioner of Italian puffery.

The original compositions are far from flawless. Overlong pedal passages bespeak the development of the composer's personal virtuosity as executant rather than his sense of proportion as builder. Repetition of subject-matter proves his joy in lovely sound rather

[1] Terry, p. 96. Illustrations of the Weimar buildings alluded to in this chapter may be found at the end of Professor Terry's book.

than his capacity to make that joy promptly communicable. Monotony of key indicates a certain lack of adventurous spirit. A few bars towards the end of the C minor Fugue, for example,[1] can only be described as athematic—meaningless emissions of sound. The mere flourish by way of ending the same fugue is as if the composer were attempting to discover a musical parallel for the pretentious flourishes of Renaissance decoration. The artificial nature of the climax and anti-climax in the Fugue in G major[2] is a sign of the will to use a lever while the fulcrum has not yet been discovered.

Some of those faults derive less from the immaturity of the composer's own craftsmanship than from the exotic ideal of the Italian music for which he probably had to pretend admiration. On the other hand, the more conscious harmonic sense of the Italians, however limited its range, added a small detail to the musical technic Bach inherited from the German tradition. Thus the long pedal passage at the beginning of the Prelude in G major is something more than a merely thematic statement, suggesting as it does the new vertical basis of music more pleasing to men who lived at the top of things, as well as the old horizontal conception which had been more pleasing to the communally-minded people.

When Bach came to the fullness of his power he

[1] Peters Edition, IV, 36; Novello, II, 48.
[2] Peter's Edition, IV, 9, bars 136 and following; Novello, VII, 80.

worked both in the horizontal tapestry of polyphony and the vertical columns of homophony; he mastered them both, and applied each to its own special and natural purpose. The more significant, therefore, that all his finest achievements prove his own preference, and the greater inherent virtue, of the earlier method.

Should further evidence of the truth of that statement be needed, the reader may be reminded of the efforts of Mozart, Beethoven, and Wagner, at the height of their powers, to recapture the craft of polyphony.

In the many-melodied style there is much more than a personal power. There is not only the sense of a mass of freely moving individuals, but also a sense of that greater unity which gives order to life, and greater freedom because of the order. There is furthermore a fascinating paradox of the expected and the surprising, like to the changing formation of birds in flight, as the moving parts are modified and accommodated to each other.

Reference has been made once or twice already to the parallel between the Gothic spirit in architecture and the polyphonic spirit in music. Both arrived at their finest expression in the heart of Christendom, the centre of Western Europe, even as the pseudo-Hellenic spirit of the Renaissance emanated from decadent Rome, and had its natural expression in prison-like forms of building and the comparatively rigid forms of homophonic music.

A glance at the Duke of Weimar's palace, the Wilhelmsburg, or the Gelbes Schloss,[1] before playing one of Bach's Vivaldi transcriptions will, I think, cause us to feel the relationship between them. The heavy earthbound solidity of the architecture is punctuated by a multitude of identically shaped windows, secured by a number of identically shaped pilasters, an occasional puerile sign added by way of ornament, lank lettering to declare the private nature of the property, and an heraldic design to proclaim the pride of its possessor.

All those things have their counterparts in the Italian music.

The dull continuity of the sound is sometimes empty of defined theme. Thus, after the opening bars of the Vivaldi-Bach Concerto in D major[2] there is not a single noteworthy musical sentence. The first three bars establish an idea of heavy earth-bound dignity, after which the movement is punctuated by sequences which, having stated a frail semblance of figure, repeat it until it is threadbare, secure the piece by pilasters of monotonous chord, and overscribble the whole with the fussiness of the fiddler who first made and played it.

At close quarters it is the flatness of the masonry, and considered bar by bar the emptiness of the music,

[1] Terry, illustrations, 37-41.
[2] No. 1 in the Peters Edition.

which are most obvious. Seen from a distance, as a
whole, both architecture and music are equally monotonous because of the vacuous repetition of such features
as they have. Such building is mere stone-piling, such
sound mere note-spinning. They are masses which have
no lifting power. They were not formed by the real
need of the general life, and cannot carry our thoughts
or feelings beyond themselves. Size of building and
length of music were dictated beforehand; no growth
of human life extended the walls, no aspiration threw
up forms of architectural beauty, no inner pressure of
the spirit of man caused lovely growth of sound from
germinal phrase to inspiring climax. The whole function and end of the Wilhelmsburg is declared at a
glance; the whole significance of the concerto-move-
ment in the first three bars.

We are told that the concertos of Vivaldi had aston-
ished the Weimar court because of 'the novelty of their
style.' That is significant of their origin and purpose.
They had no other function than to kill time more or
less politely, and time is never to be killed by good
works of art. If art-works have any heart, time is made
more alive by them; if art-works are heartless they
make us the more time-conscious. But from the period
of the Renaissance until to-day, leisure-class art has
had for its primary business the relief of boredom by
helping to make people forgetful of time. Of course it
has never succeeded in that object, for all capable artists

THE WILHELMSBURG, WEIMAR

have opposed such a conception of their work; but their opposition has not altered the fact.

Nothing grows old so quickly as works produced for the sake of their novelty, and so soon as the art has been staled for its patrons, it has been discarded in favour of a later vogue. The shrewd tradesmen who make big successes in the art business have been those who made it their job to provide novelty at all costs, and always more of it.

The art-tradesmen of the Renaissance achieved novelty by ignoring the original expressive value of the arts, by ceasing to use them as a great common possession, by degrading them to the level of personal pride —the pride of the solitary rich possessor, the pride of the solitary clever technician. Builders were turned from the great common house with its one great room to the private and personal houses of men who demanded many rooms and many storeys; and they signed them with their patrons' initials and heraldic designs instead of the common and more varied signs with which the earlier masons had enriched the whole life of their time.

So, also, the men who made music for those who lived in big houses were turned from the great common songs of the people, and the polyphonic variety which the people had once learned to weave about such songs, and instructed to juggle foolishly with notes as a circus-clown would juggle more admirably with knives.

After the multivarious life of the people had been excluded from the arts, skill and then reason faded out; musicians achieved unity of style by absence of original theme, builders by absence of original design. They made a virtue of flat empty surfaces because such served more effectively as backgrounds for personal posturing and pretentiousness. They had to acquire a sufficient skill in masonry and note-building to ensure temporary standing power for their works. Therein was their only right to the name of artists. It was a meaner dignity than the name of artisan in the Middle Ages. Judging by the disappearance of the music, and the weakness of a good deal of the building, especially as an active influence, even that right was often dishonestly won.[1]

Such was the art which was best liked by the ruling class, the patrons for musicians in Bach's Germany. That was the kind of service expected of our musician at Weimar, if he would make a success of his career.

Behind Bach, however, and within him, was a great creative force against which he could no more prevail than Balaam could prevail against the angel. Bach's genius was the ass which kept him in the right way, even as he strove to follow up a more easy and profitable career. Let us consider the nature of that genius, and range it against his few parlour tricks.

[1] Recall the case of rubble for stone-work discovered a few years ago when Wren's St. Paul's was found to be insecure.

The mass of a great Gothic building is actually more earth-bound than that of a Renaissance building by reason of the buttresses which secure it; but those buttresses appear to hold it down, not as the roots of a tree, but as if they were the anchorage of some monstrous air-ship. The character of Gothic lines is such that, from cottage gable to cathedral spire, the thoughts of the onlooker are carried upwards. It seems to say, Here we are on this earth of ours, and here we must stay; but what we can touch is not the whole of life; there above are rolling fires and floating worlds, blue rapture of space and wild wrath of cloud, the roofing of our home through which vanishes the smoke of our hearths, from which fall the water of life and the flash of death.

Excluding all superstitions of a heaven beyond space, it is certain enough that not only important scientific discovery, but aesthetic imagination and other refinements of the human mind have their birth and growth in star-gazing and sky-dreaming.

The original and useful functions of Christian buildings were obvious, and could be taken for granted; but that was not enough. So long as Christian civilization was in a condition of healthy growth men were in a state of mental alertness, experimenting and exploring. Of that part of their characters the Gothic roofs are an architectural sign and symbol, straining into the most mysterious part of nature with the vision of artists and the will of scientists.

On the other hand, in Renaissance architecture the roof is a detail of apparent indifference. Those whose chief aim was material wealth, and political power to ensure that wealth, had no use for an expensive and useless struggle towards the sky. Galileo the scientist was imprisoned, Dante the artist accused of financial dishonesty by a usurious and simoniacal priesthood, and the people brought into a new form of slavery, at the same time that popular forms of architecture were discarded. Those who feared to explore the facts of nature and the stimulating force of artistic imagination rejected the roof which shot up heavenward. A Renaissance roof was built against the climate, and that was all, with the amusing consequence that it promptly expressed the absurd and mean characters of its builders. When small it reminds one of the tiny hat of a music-hall comedian; when it swells into domes it looks bloated like the tumour on St. Paul's of London, or ridiculous like the pimple on the palace of Bach's master at Weimar.

That meanness evidently struck some of the more pretentious Renaissance builders, so they occasionally indulged in an open-air gallery of gods on their house-tops: gods skied there because they were *not* believed in, either as objective existences, or as symbols of influences friendly or hostile to those who lived beneath.

The horizontal mass of the Wilhelmsburg proclaimed its indifference to anything beyond itself. Its proportions were settled before it was built. Its mood is that of men who have settled down—*down*. But the proportions of even the homeliest gable cottage are up-sweeping as to roof-line, and *un*settled, inasmuch as the cottager used always to have the hope of future additions to house the growth of his family and wealth. That same sense of growth informed the noblest examples of Gothic building, and resulted in the infinite variety which is their most striking physical attribute. As for Christian tower and steeple—think not only of their visible imaginative values, but also of the bell-play within them. Those belfries declare the rapturous excess of a common wealth which had moved the builders to luxury and launched them into the last of the arts, the art of music.

Roof is necessary. Pinnacles, towers, and steeples will only be added when life is so rich that men must spend their labour on lovely and needless things. Then, when every general idea has been symbolised in sculpture, detailed in painting, and explained in literary art, the overflow of rational hope and irrational joy must find irrational expression in rational form. That is why music is the last art to develop[1] in the uprise of civilizations, and the first art to suffer in their decline.

However high the roof springs it is based on the foundations; and the more carefully the foundations are laid the higher the roof may rise. Likewise, however irrationally the music may flourish it originates in the

---

[1] Professor Flinders Petrie, *The Revolutions of Civilisation.*

facts of life; and the more deeply the facts relate to a common human joy the more strongly the music may soar.

At first the music is but an emphasis of verbal expression, as colour-painting is at first the emphasis of graven outline and scriven word. But gradually the later arts gather strength until they culminate in a Giotto or a Bach. Then, in their final expression, colour and tone find emotional languages of their own; and they are able, not only to reinforce the ideas of the lines and words with which they are associated, not only to add ideas for which uncoloured line and spoken word are inadequate, but able to exist separately in their own loveliness of colour-scheme and instrumental music. In this last phase the two most delicate arts seem, like Gothic steeples, to strain into an impossible world—seem to seek a condition of complete and impossible freedom, even as Ariel was for ever trying to escape from the humane service and intellectual discipline of Prospero:

ARIEL:

> Is there more toil? Since thou dost give me pains,
> Let me remember thee what thou hast promised
> Which is not yet performed me.

PROSPERO:

> How now, moody?
> What is't thou canst demand?

ARIEL:

> My liberty.

GOTHIC V. RENAISSANCE IN MUSIC

PROSPERO:
> Before the time be out? No more.

Stone bursts into fire in flamboyant tracery; pictorial art into impressionism as in the paintings of Turner; poetry into music as in the verse of Poe; and music into air, in the spiritual flights or fugues of Bach; and all these things have virtue so long as they have submitted to the necessary discipline and have joy in human service.

Of all man's attempts to reach a purely spiritual condition it is in the art of music that he has most completely succeeded; but even music cannot survive as a vital and intelligible art if it is continually and completely cut off from its original vocal associations. Bach's most spiritual flights in pure tone were possible because they sprang from an age-long tradition which was grounded in the songs of the people. The German chorale was to the fugue what foundations and buttresses were to the cathedral belfry. So it is that people who have studied the vocal works of Bach, and their obvious and consistent connection with the chorale, will the more easily appreciate his instrumental works; whereas those who approach Bach through the latter are placed at some disadvantage, and it is no uncommon thing to hear such people describe the instrumental music as a sort of glorified five-finger exercise. So it is; but they don't really see the glory, or the finger exercise would not occur to them.

Recalling the rhythm of the windows around the Wilhelmsburg and its counterpart in the dull sequences of Vivaldi, we must remember that the main outlines of a fine Gothic building are not punctuated, but inter-related by means of a network of subordinate structural lines, and embroidered with a mass of detail which enriches the whole, but does not mean much to an on-looker who may be regarding the building from a distance. So also a Bach fugue is crosswoven with the structural lines of its voices, and enriched by a mass of detail which a mere listener does not hear. The virtue of the unseen carving in the building, and of the unheard phrases in the fugue, lies in the fact that the one was chiselled by the creative hand of a common workman, the other intended for an ordinary chorus-singer or orchestral player. They are arts for doers, rather than for onlookers and listeners.

But human degradation was the key-note of the Duke of Weimar's religion. The majority of performers of music in the Italian tradition were enslaved as the common builders were enslaved in the erection of Renaissance architecture. If the mere acceptance of labour as mason or fiddler in such work is not a sign of degradation, the activity will itself ensure a degrading process.

Renaissance workmen were at first not allowed, and were finally incapable of, the imaginative effort necessary for the production of a considerable mass of inter-

esting detail. Architect and soloist might still retain
self-respect as artists, but not the common masons and
musicians.

The best that could be done by the architects of
those Weimar palaces was to pick out the least degraded
of their masons to sculpt an heraldic design—which he
has done with all the fat nastiness of Renaissance ideal-
ism—and perhaps copy the figures of a few Greek gods,
whose forms he could not freshly create any more than
he could imagine the divine powers of which they were
the symbols.

A similar degradation was overtaking the rank and
file of musicians in Bach's time. They were no longer
taking part in the varied equality of polyphony. They
were now required to play tum-tum accompaniments
while a few favoured creatures disported themselves in
solo parts. The sport was a vain one: vain in that it
developed mental attributes which have often made
even distinguished musicians the mock of sane men;
vain also, inasmuch as the majority of concertos and
pieces in which there are predominant parts for soloists,
vocal or instrumental, are generally empty of deep pur-
port, often mere noise and nothingness.

The curse of such solo-vanity has blasted the musical
art of Italy to this day. For lack of the deeper issues
which arise in the clash and comradeship of communal
effort, Italian music since the days of Palestrina has
been almost uniformly dull and petty, except where it

has reached out towards the average mind in certain vulgar and sensational operas. The affectedly higher forms of art have been tolerable only as means of personal display. When we listen to an artist like Kreisler playing the stuff we may be seduced into thinking it fine because of the personality of the player and the sensuous beauty of the sounds he makes. As transcribed by Bach for keyed instruments we are left to ourselves to make of it what we can. The German master has given the show away.

Had Bach wanted to expose to his duke the meanness of the Italian music he could not have taken a more likely course. Had the duke been a true music-lover he would have realised how little such music had to say as compared with the pieces which his servant was still drawing from the original German fount. But that sort of master doesn't want music to say anything as a rule. Art which had said things in the past, and especially popular art, had generally been rude to the governing class. As Henry VIII suppressed monasteries and mystery plays, as a traitor-priesthood obliterated with whitewash the wall paintings of artisans, so the Duke of Weimar banished the native music of Germany: it was inevitably associated with ideas prejudicial to his own authority. Much better for him and his like a fat amiable fussing of sound.

Bach even transcribed concertos by the duke's own nephew. They are numbers eleven and sixteen of those usually attributed to Vivaldi, and are little worse than their models.

Only a slave-driving or an enslaved brain could have been content with that prison-like or factory-like aspect of Renaissance wall, broken by primitive symbol, branded with master's initials, and secured architecturally by methods of the mere copyist. And the degradation which accompanies slavery is obvious in the poverty of skill employed. The amazing skill which sent Gothic vaulting curving like arrows may be compared with the lesser skill needed for the laying of Renaissance entablature upon shaft; the amazing skill which sent those vari-coloured threads of melody flying together in easily disciplined association with the lesser skill needed for the planning of figuration over chord.

Such signs of slavery and degradation are evident in the flat walls of the Duke of Weimar's palaces, in the empty circles on either side of the doorway of the Gelbes Schloss, and in the debased Ionic capitals of its pillars. No less of enslavement is to be found in the flat dullness of the Vivaldi music with its petty themes and narrow range of chord structure.

That Bach suffered real slavery, temporary degradation of his own natural power, is evident in his Vivaldi transcriptions, though perhaps it is not easy for the majority of people to understand that. It was as if a skilled letter writer were condemned to the making of pothooks, a skilled joiner to the chopping of firewood, a skilled electrician to the stoking of furnaces.

Compare the petty invention and degrading copy-work of the Vivaldi transcriptions with even an early work of Bach's own. It is as if we turned from the Wilhelmsburg and faced Chartres cathedral; as if we glanced from the headlines of a child's copybook to an illuminated thirteenth century missal. Flatness and tentativeness and monotony have given place to variety, fullness, mastery, and surprise. And even as the monotony of the Italian offered no real rest, so the surprise of the Gothic music creates no disturbance of feeling.

Vivaldi repeated his sequences till they were threadbare, though his figures were seldom worth a second hearing, much less a fifth and sixth; and it is hard to say of his themes which are chief, which derivative.

Sequential treatment was an important part of Bach's decorative method also. In his early works there are sequences of figure which are unrolled nearly to the length of a Vivaldi example. Even so they do not make the same monotonous effect, because the detail is more distinguished and yet subordinated to the work as a whole. They often spring out of the main subjects, but never pretend to be a main subject. They are decorative fragments, incidental but germane to the development of the main thought.

The Italian musician's sequences make an effect as of persons painted in a picture several times over that they may not be overlooked in their mediocrity. The German master's sequences are as of rhythms in certain subordinate details of a picture—a series of clouds or a chain of distant mountain-tops. When Bach treated the more essential parts of his musical structure in a sequential way he rarely extended the passage beyond a double sequence; if a third statement is begun it is generally turned into a fresh channel before it is completed.

Bach's fugues had the same relation to his chief works that Beethoven's bagatelles had to his. Bach's earliest fugues were trial flights for the soaring work which lay before him. His later fugues were generally joy-rides, for love of the sensation of musical flight, and love of the skill he had in the management of his flying machine; a few of them were descents into hell.

From the prison of Renaissance artifice Bach escaped by means of his art into the living air. His art remained Gothic in spirit even when he tried to carry out his master's will. His great contemporary, Handel, having a more pliable genius, was able to turn easily from German polyphony to Italian homophony; but his art suffered inevitable degradation when he accepted the meaner task, and Handel never acquired the ultimate skill or the depth of Bach.

One of the results of the change was an impoverishment of harmony. The very art which professed to have a harmonic rather than a melodic basis proved itself in that, as in other ways, inferior to the Gothic spirit which it supplanted in fashionable favour. But the variety of Bach's chords is as striking as his variety of form in other respects.

The dull pillars of chord in the Vivaldi concertos were piled because the musician knew beforehand exactly what they were going to be. He chose his chords and raised his work upon them, as the builder of the Gelbes Schloss had known what an Ionic column was, and copied it over and over again to the best of his ability. The poor Renaissance architect had but three varieties of column to choose from; and, curiously enough, the Italian used chiefly three chords, two at a time.

However, though the architectonic balance maintained by Bach is even more satisfactory than that of Vivaldi, Bach's chords, like the pillars of a Gothic cathedral, happened as and when they were required by the general structure; and the master did *not* know what they were going to be beforehand. Gothic pillars flowered in the multi-variety of their capitals; Bach's chords by reason of the comparative freedom of his parts. In that way they have the inherent life alluded to by Forster when he describes the characters of Dickens' novels: 'the intensity of his observation of individual humours and vices had taken so many varieties of imaginative form. Everything in *Chuzzlewit* had indeed grown under treatment, as will commonly be the case in the handling of a man of genius, who never knows where any given conception may lead him, out of the wealth of resource in development and incident which it has itself created.'

Exactly similar was the art of Bach. Sometimes he, like the Italians, used his chords in couples deliberately —tonic and dominant, or tonic and subdominant. We see an example of that in the episode figure of the early D major prelude for organ. Occasionally, indeed, a single chord contented him, for a short space, as at the climax of the D major Fugue. But generally speaking, the fact that Bach did not know what chords he would hear, until the weaving of the parts informed him, resulted in a much richer harmonic texture.

Later on he deliberately explored the possibilities of the harmonic basis of music. The *Chromatic Fantasia* offers an example of such exploration. Then he discovered a harmonic wealth of which the Italians had no conception; but even so he discovered less than he had already lighted on by accident in the ordering of his polyphony.

During his earlier period as composer, and in the first flush of his creative power, he was mainly intent on musical expression, and used the traditional method which cost least conscious effort. In that phase, and in all his best work, harmony was not in itself an expressional factor so much as a discipline, enabling him to adjust the differences arising between his parts, as they pursued their comparatively free ways in the communal music. To have given greater latitude to the harmonic principle would have left the music at the autocratic mercy of the one of the parts, the others being disciplined by the harmony into accord with that single part. That is what the Italians were doing.

On the other hand, to have neglected altogether the discipline of harmony would have meant anarchy as between the parts, so hindering the attainment of that euphony which is generally regarded as the mark of the noblest works of man. That is what many self-conscious modern composers are doing.

A conception which admits the need for real living expression in art, necessitates the discipline of harmony. A conception which admits also the maximum of freedom for every individual engaged, prevents the discipline from becoming tyrannical and stultifying.

Euphony in the Christian arts persisted so long as Christian principles were accepted in life. That euphony pervaded all that Bach wrote from first to last.

Renaissance artists sought pleasure for their goal, even when they held by the conventional Christian symbols. For Christian artists, even of Renaissance period and training—men like Botticelli, Byrd, and Milton—Christian ideas and realities were the goal, pleasure but an incident.

Pleasure was the only purpose of the Vivaldi concertos, and of the ducal court which preferred them, however religious the duke may have wished to be. Apart from the sensuous beauty of the music, the chief interest of those pieces depends upon the cleverness of the solo-fiddler, and not upon the musical phrases, or upon their emotional significance which is but small.

The instrumental solos of Bach had a deeper value, partly because they originated in a vocal style which was associated with the choral will and the straightforward tunes of the people; and were developed upon communal principles, even when the medium was the autocratic organ. Occasionally it appears as if Bach were drawing attention to the skill of the performer, especially in the pedal work of his early organ pieces; but it is clear that he avoided the dull vanity of the Italians, by making virtuosity itself a means of humorous expression. Even as he exerted his skill he laughed at himself.

Vivaldi and his fellows had settled down to a cold and calculating game of skill. Bach roused himself for a circus performance. Thus in his C major Prelude he capered on the organ like a clown on a dancing elephant, and for the fugue that follows he provided a subject with a quick octave leap, as sudden and as merry as the winking of an eyelid.

Nor is Bach's superiority to his own skill the only proof of the superiority of that skill. He does things of *hidden* virtuosity which no Italian would or could have attempted, either at that time or since. Vivaldi ad-

ventured like an elderly man learning to ride a push-
bike: he got up a moderate speed and then kept to the
by-roads. Bach went everywhere, along high roads and
by-roads, up hill, down dale, and even (as we shall see
later on) into my lady's chamber. In the tenth bar from
the end of the C major organ Prelude he plunged reck-
lessly into a thornbush of dissonance; in the thirty-
first bar of the same piece he squeezed F against E and
D against C sharp with all the assurance of the adven-
turer, and all the gaiety of a medieval mason carving
a gargoyle.

Such was the kind of music which Bach made within
the walls of the Wilhelmsburg for a prince whose religious will was law for his clergy, and whose musical
will was for second-rate concertos from Italy.

Doubtless from the duke's point of view the Italian
school was good because it achieved unity of style and
an affectation of refined intellectuality without expressing anything definite, and therefore without expressing
anything dangerous. Unlike those popular chorales it
was entirely removed from the realities of life.

The young organist may have tried to prove the good
faith of his service by making those transcriptions, and
even by temporarily abjuring the use of the chorale in
his own works. But we cannot help suspecting that the
duke looked with some suspicion upon the original
works, full of revolt as they were against all that the
Vivaldi music signified.

Bach was obliged to do his lackey-service; but his own fertile and turbulent genius was too strong to accept dictation from an authority which was without authenticity. The early organ works of Bach are full of faults, though we should scarcely be aware of the fact unless we had his later works to judge by—as full of faults as were the great Gothic cathedrals. But neither cathedrals nor fugues have the mortal fault of expressionlessness, like the dead walls of the Gelbes Schloss and the deadly dull bars of the Italian concertos by Vivaldi and the Duke of Weimar's nephew.

With all their faults Bach's early organ pieces were vital. The composer was a man with an original outlook —that is to say, he looked for his artistic basis to the origins of religious faith and musical skill. Consequently he was unable to quench the original dramatic fires of his art. He could no more avoid the dramatic possibilities of music than he could damp down the fires of his own vitality.

At Weimar Bach's mouth was closed so far as clear utterance of Christian ideas was concerned. But the cause was alive in his heart; and in his own instrumental works we find him, not making pretty musical speeches in the Italian style to please his master, as he could so easily have done, and in later times actually did—but striving with the dramatic possibilities of his musical medium.

So long as he associated that language with the popular and definite concepts of the chorale there was no mistaking its meaning. Later, in his Cantatas and Passions, that meaning became even clearer. In his instrumental works the objective is not so obvious, because it has seemed to many as if he were studying to develop music as a detached art. But we have already seen that no such music can hang together except upon a purely formal basis. It is the more significant therefore, that Bach should have written pieces which owe their shape to forces other than the architectonic laws of absolute and decorative music. Other such pieces, and finer ones, were soon to come; and the more we study the great series of chorale-preludes and choral works (especially the Passions and chorale-cantatas, which formed the most essential part of his life-work) the more we realize that the instrumental works of his Weimar period were exercises by means of which he learned to use the language of music in a dramatic manner.

Six years after Bach was appointed organist to the Duke of Weimar he was promoted to be Concertmaster. From that time his attitude grows clearer to us, because the new position entailed the composition of church-cantatas.

The manner of his promotion is not without interest. He had competed, and was chosen, for the position of organist for the Church of Our Lady at Halle. After considering the matter for about a month he decided against taking up that appointment, much to the annoyance of the Halle officials who accused him of using them, to better his conditions at Weimar. Judging by Bach's actions there may have been some ground for the taunt; but other things also affected his decision. The terms of the agreement which he would have been obliged to sign showed that the religious strife he had experienced in Mühlhausen existed at Halle also. Moreover the agreement included items to which no artist could easily subscribe. They proposed not only to dictate the channels of his artistic expression, but the very organ-stops he should use for the hymns; though, to do the Halle people justice, it is possible that the taste of previous organists had rendered such a stipulation necessary. Then, of course, there was the inevitable opposition from the Duke of Weimar, who was in a position to hold his menial to his own service. And that was probably the decisive factor for, in a subsequent letter written by the composer to the Halle officials in defence of his behaviour, he said that, altogether apart from matters of salary, he was unable to change his situation owing to a question of law. That the Halle people came to understand the affair in that light seems likely by reason of an invitation they sent him later on. The invitation, to examine and report on a new organ, he accepted, and was treated as a very honoured guest.

If it was the duke who had stood in the way, he evidently tried to make it up to Bach—not necessarily in financial terms, for Halle had offered him less than he was already getting at Weimar; but by giving the musician opportunities for composition in larger forms—such opportunities as had perhaps been hitherto unduly monopolised by the inferior musician who was Bach's official superior.

Chapter Seven

IMPRISONED

CHRISTIANITY and the common life of the people had already been intimately associated in Bach's earliest cantatas; and, as we have already seen, not only in the occasions for which they had been written, but also, and more significantly, in the chorale-stuff which permeated them and the polyphony which gave them communal form.

Even at Weimar, before he had been officially required to produce such things, he had made two church-cantatas; and, so far as can be ascertained, they were composed without previous commission, possibly even without a definite performance in view.

Both works not only prove the master's comparative steadfastness to his original principles—they also reveal something of his mental life and personal feelings during his court service.

The cantata, *Nach dir, Herr verlanget mich,* is evidently an outcry of personal suffering. The words express the feelings of one who is troubled by the course his life has taken.

There is a short sorrowful instrumental introduction, based upon the downward chromatic figure already used in the farewell to his brother, a figure regularly used by Bach for the expression of extreme suffering, and eventually used for the *Crucifixus* in the B minor Mass.

Next a chorus in which the same figure persists:

> Lord, my soul doth thirst for Thee!
> O God, my hope is in Thee!
> Let me never be confounded.
> Up, Lord, that my foes may not triumph over me!

Then a more hopeful aria asserting that 'right is and will be always right.' In that aria is a little detail which is amusing in its betrayal of a major quality in the composer's own character. To the words 'no worldly care shall move me' the music suddenly pauses in its polyphonic progress, and sticks upon a single chord with the obstinacy which was an outstanding part of his own nature when engaged in his several disputes. That feeling grows in the next section of the cantata into an assurance that because his point of view is right it will finally be vindicated:

> 'Stablish me upon the rock of truth
> And comfort me;
> For the Lord is God, my hope and strength.

The music develops: instead of an obstinate monochord we have a steady upward scale passing from part to part —a symbol of right forcing its way up starkly through all adversity; and when the scale rises beyond vocal convenience, it is taken over by the less personal and more powerful tones of the orchestra. Could there be a more exact symbol in music of the idea presented by the words—the ultimate impersonal vindication of truth, a truth which is at present beyond a single man's power to assert? And then the parts state their separate trust in what the future will bring forth.

The whole mood changes, and the people's song enters into one of the loveliest forms with which it has ever been clothed by a great artist. It sings that ultimate faith in the good purpose of life without which no man can do good work, whether the work be the ploughing of the field or the fashioning of a chorus:

> Cedars on the mountains swaying
> Bow their heads the winds obeying,
> Proudly o'er the tempests ride.
> Hearken thou to Gods commanding
> Though it pass thy understanding:
> Trust in Him whate'er betide.

Bach's head had already often had to bow to the harsh wind of evil circumstance—ducal anger of burgherish blockheadedness—but the genius within him, which had been originally derived from just such popular songs as this, ever insisted on uttering the crucial word, and it seems that not even Bach himself was able to prevent it. However inconvenient that inner genius of his may have been in the matter of his personal advancement, it gave him a power which enabled him to work on defiantly, though in mental chains, to the end of his days, and filled him with that strange happiness which has been recorded of artists who have lived even more suppressed lives than he.

So, in significant opposition to the first sad chorus, the one which follows that assertion of the spirit of the people is a song of joy. The themes are now of an ascending tendency, and though no actual phrase of folk-song is used the flavour of the chorale is present throughout. And the real thing breaks through again in the last number of the cantata—a chorale-chaconne:

> Though my life be only sadness
> God will end my days in gladness.
> Jesus head with thorns was crowned,
> But his joy in heaven abounded.
> So in God my hope is stayed
> Of men's power unafraid
> Christ the dead, yet in us living
> Gives us victory in our striving.[1]

The last chorus thus revives the spirit of the popular and materialistic Christianity of the Middle Ages. That spirit is to some extent obscured by the symbolic phraseology; but the final lines mean nothing intelligible if they do not proclaim that the real Christ is alive, not in the skies, but in living men on earth; so there is still a chance of ultimate victory in a more real sense than was encouraged by orthodox Lutheranism.

[1] The above translations by Steuart Wilson have been quoted from Messrs. Breitkopf and Härtel's English edition.

The significance of this cantata in relation to the
time and conditions of its composition is clear enough.
Therefore we need not be surprised to learn that an attempt has been made to deny it as a work of Bach's.
If it were conceivable that there were two such composers alive just then (and Rubinstein said the day
would come when men would believe that Bach's works
were written, not by one but by many) the absence of
this cantata would take an important link from the personal aspect of this study. It would leave us a little less
clear regarding Bach's own feelings during the Weimar
period, and we should miss a rung in the ladder of his
descent from optimism. The 'happy ending,' so much
derided by some people, is one of the surest signs of a
healthy and creative spirit. But the loss of this cantata
would enormously add to our major argument, that the
art of Bach was no mere result of a personal and
dividual genius, but essentially individual, original, and
communal.

The other ducally unauthorised cantata was *Gottes
Zeit*. It is said to be a funeral music; but was not, Spitta
declares, intended for any member of the duke's
own family. 'It has a depth and intensity of expression
which reach the extreme limits of possibility of representation by music. The arrangement of the poetic
material is most excellent. . . . In several fit and expressive thoughts which are freely interspersed we can
almost recognise Bach's own hand. If such be the case

the whole arrangement of the poetry may with reason be ascribed to him.'

Not only was this text almost certainly Bach's own, but that of the cantata previously described in this chapter. Indeed, I cannot help feeling that the composer was responsible for more of his texts than is generally imagined. We know that he modified details and made substantial additions to librettos by other men. And there is the singular manner in which many of them apply to the religious life of the time and to his personal career—apply, not with such an application as would have been given by an orthodox librettist, but exactly according to Bach's own pietist bias. Moreover, we cannot help noticing that it is in some of his most expressive works that the authorship is in doubt.

It is in just such works as this *Gottes Zeit*, wherein the consecutiveness of the movements unfolds a dramatic idea—an idea which is in harmony with his general mental development, and more strongly expressed than in the work of any known contemporary—that the deeper parts of the master's nature are most likely to be revealed.

Strangely entitled *Actus Tragicus*, this cantata has been looked upon as a funeral music. If so, it is for no ordinary ceremony. No artist, and especially no artist with so realistic a mind as Bach, would give such a title for a cantata made for a customary death-rite, not for his dearest friend, and certainly not for the death of a royal person.

Not only the title, but the loving perfection of artistry which was devoted to its making, proves that it was specially important in the composer's own mind. Then, in connection with the contention that Bach constantly associated the people's songs with the popular conception of the Christian religion, it would appear as though the tragic drama here expressed might be the failure and funeral of Christianity itself.

Consider some of its detail: Unrelenting sternness in the first half, expressive of the mysterious life which passes human understanding, a prayer for mental discipline, and a command for organization. In that earlier half is an attitude of determinism, of resignation to inevitable destiny. And throughout that part there is no suggestion of chorale. But when the work reaches the happier moment when individual human beings take conscious part in the rite—then at once the people's song appears.

Nevertheless the part to be played by human beings is no longer the real and material thing which it had been in earlier times; nor is there even the veiled hope suggested in the previous cantata.

Here in the *Actus Tragicus* we have another retreat in the fight against actual wrong. The hope that

> Christ the dead in us yet living
> Gives us victory in our striving,

is evidently not so strong as it was. It is hard to remain steadfast in a series of battles which seem every time to be won by the forces of wrong—a war in which even those who most suffer are easily decoyed into the service of the enemy. Is there no way of sustaining the battle without bringing on one's self a violence which may shortly make it impossible to fight at all? Can a man appear to give in, and yet continue to serve the cause of righteousness in other, and perhaps secret, ways? Many good folk were already doing that; and some such modification of religious outlook seems to be indicated by the *Actus Tragicus*.

Perhaps the funeral which it celebrated was the sacrifice of the composer's own career; perhaps it was the death of Christianity itself in a real and material sense —the sacrifice or end of the outward struggle, and its transference to a spiritual and imaginative sphere.

Especially revealing in that connection is the little duet in which the voice of Jesus promises Paradise *subsequent* to death, and the tired Christian promptly accepts death as a precious gift, superior to life itself. 'Into Thy hands I commend my spirit' and 'To-day thou shalt be with Me in Paradise,' phrases chosen by Bach himself, perfectly express his own mental desires in a world where all the noblest functions of his art were denied; where his imagination could only be asserted in art-forms to which the general public had no access. The only hope that remained was the unreal world called Paradise.

Sir Thomas More had been faced with the same disappointment when he wrote his *Utopia*, Milton when he wrote *Paradise Lost*, Bunyan when he wrote *Pilgrims' Progress*. As they, so Bach, whose *Actus Tragicus* expressed the position in which all Christians found themselves—at least all who had believed and laboured that the Great Kingdom might really come on earth.

Another detail of much meaning in the cantata was a cause of stumbling for Spitta, who said the work was undramatic because of the very number of forms in which the dramatic sense is most fully shown. The greater mass of the chorus—altos, tenors, and basses—sing the inevitability of death: 'It is the Old Decree, Man thou art mortal.' Against that from time to time the sopranos cry for the coming of Christ. The orchestral material is inlaid with a chorale[1] which indicates unuttered words which would be understood by some at least of those who might hear it. Those unuttered words related to the final abandonment of the life struggle, and the complete casting of the self upon the forces of circumstance.

After trying to solve that riddle with the key of orthodoxy, Spitta was brought up against the fact that the music does not enforce, but denies the idea that the curse of death has been changed into blessing by the

[1] Ich hab'mein Sach' Gott heimgestellt.

coming of Christ. So Bach, even as he proposed to transfer the Kingdom of God to a remote future after death,
expressed his incredulity.

For people who are comfortably off in this world the
legend of a far-off heaven for 'believers' and men of
'good deeds' may seem well enough, especially if their
belief is sufficiently vague, and the nature of good deeds
not too clearly defined. But what about those who suffer
want and pain on earth? What about Bach himself in his
invidious position—in the outer world a demand for
shameful service (remember the general character of
those German courts), and within the accusing voice of
his own popular and pietist genius!

Had Bach or anyone else a real assurance that Christian principles would win in death what they had failed
to win from life?

Spitta proposed a comparison of musico-dramatic
treatment which will serve us equally well. 'Gluck
makes the Furies retreat gradually before the song of
Orpheus and leave the field to him; in Bach the threat-
ening image of the Old Decree remains to the last,' as it
was in very fact surviving in Bach's time everywhere.

The meaning of that almost secret use of the people's
song is surely clear enough. Its free and open use in the
numbers which follow is associated entirely with the
imaginative and unreal nature of Christian ideas transferred to a world of dream.

Those chorale-founded numbers are further examples

of the bondage and sympathies of an artist who even in
his bondage was clearly reaching out to the masses of
the people. Bach spoke mystically from his prison-house
at Weimar as Bunyan from Bedford jail. He had come
to terms with hard fact. His family was fast increasing;
if he would be fair to his wife and children he must
be resigned to the prison-house of mysticism for his
art. For Christ was a hard master, and, if any man went
to Him, and hated not his father, and mother, and wife,
and children, and brethren, and sisters, yea, and his
own life also,' he could not fully serve Him.

Uninfluenced by the taste or will of his paymaster
Bach wrote the two cantatas we have just considered.
Now we have to examine works in similar form which
were composed for the edification of a lordling who
himself decided points of religious difference, after
amenable university professors had devilled his briefs.

A certain change is at once apparent. 'Instead of dramatic texts we now get wretched poems which are always cut out to the same pattern. The arioso is
supplanted by the da capo aria and the secco recitative.
The plan is still further impoverished by the fact that
the choir now recedes wholly into the background; it
figures only at the beginning and the end.'[1] Schweitzer
is puzzled and concerned by the change because from
the outset he has approved the Italian influence as de-
sirable and fruitful. But the evils he enumerates are

[1] Schweitzer, II, 127.

the result of the master's acceptance of foreign formulas which had nothing to express of the popular Christian cause in Germany, and nothing to say to the German people which concerned their welfare.

Because Bach was by that time further removed from the popular spirit whence sprang his own originality, he had to fit himself to formulas; and the formulas he chose were necessarily those dictated by the tastes of his duke. Because the composer's own emotions were the less stirred he was content with a dry recitative where formerly his creative spirit bubbled over with arioso. Because his lackey-service tended to dividuality and isolation of spirit, to the loss of those greater emotions which only reach full expression in art when a fair relation exists between artists and their fellow workmen, the coro-dramatic form which was yet to be his greatest glory received a definite set-back.

The two earlier Weimar cantatas progress from idea to idea, from emotion to emotion, with the natural consecutiveness of a living experience. It is not merely brain-logic that threads them, but the pulse of life which beats in them. And while Bach was revealing the inmost working of the human heart, he linked it up with an appeal to the reason by means of the words, and to the external physical life by means of his realistic phraseology. The quivering of the very flesh in the music for 'In Him live and move,' the figure of the startled body and its resistance to the death-summons, the last gasp of the lungs—those, and other hints of a physical nature, complete the dramatic appeal by relating the material to the intellectual and emotional world where finally the most intense strife takes place.

Already in the early chorale-variations we have seen that realistic phraseology employed to enforce the emotional expression of Christian belief. We have also seen how in the earlier preludes and fugues for organ he tried to give vital form to dramatic ideas which are beyond our power to interpret, because we are without a key such as we have to the cantatas in their texts, and to the chorale-preludes in the original words of the hymn-tunes. We have seen how in the earliest Weimar cantatas a definite emotional progress is recorded in complicated but clear form, giving in *Nach dir* the drama of Christian Life suffering oppression but not without hope of final victory, and in the *Actus Tragicus* the drama of Christian Death, associated with the forlorn hope that what is lost on earth may be gained in the sky.

It seems as if a form was being evolved for the drama which moved Bach so strongly, a form which confuses even as it impresses those who study his work.

Drama is action, but not necessarily or entirely physical action. The last faint breath of life, expressed in *Gottes Zeit* by means of a delicate musical phrase, is as truly dramatic as the death-spasms of a Shakespearean hero; Bach's response for the soul as truly dramatic as

Eliza Dolittle's swear-bomb in her mother-in-law's drawing-room. A different medium—a slower and less physical medium was used by the composer; but psychological action and reference to the most intense human experience are even more obvious in musical form, and quite as clearly conveyed as physical reactions by gesture drama and intellectual ideas by spoken drama.

Bach's own genius had led him to such dramatic expression, though before his time the popular religious drama had been suppressed. So, when he was free to choose his own texts, a dramatic basis was inevitable. When, later on, he became once more his own master (in the mental world, anyhow) he found the dramatic form he was seeking. But for the rest of his years at Weimar he was prevented from developing his natural genius, because he was supplied with castrated texts by the duke's own orthodox verse-makers.

The dramatic form which Bach had proposed, and then dropped for a time, was the same which Beethoven developed later in his instrumental works and Wagner in his stage works. It had for its prime purpose the expression of the complete mental life in the only medium capable of giving that life full expression— thoughts verbally delivered, emotions made present in music.

Had Bach been concerned with a stage presentation of his dramatic ideas he would clearly have cast them in other forms; but the stage is not the only, and not al-

ways the best means of dramatic expression; and because he had not the stage, with all that accompanies
it of physical detail, he supplied what was necessary of
the physical world by means of his realistic musical
phrases.

Such had been his creative attitude hitherto; such
was his attitude to be, and even more emphatically, in
the Passions; but during his latter years at Weimar he
tried on the foreign cloak of Renaissance artifice. From
time to time we catch sight of the real Bach within
the cloak, the worried musician in the outfit of a brigand;
and the good German is so obviously ashamed and dis-
concerted by his foreign gear that the dramatic consecutiveness of his work is completely spoiled.

For English students the later Weimar cantatas most
easily accessible are *Ich hatte viel Bekümmerniss;*[1]
Nun Komm, der Heiden Heiland;[2] *Tritt auf die Glau-
bensbahn;*[3] and one secular piece. These show a steady
increase of superiority to the Italians in the use of their
own methods, a steady increase in the element of
amusement, and a steady decrease of religious spirit.

We have already examined in the earlier cantatas
the effect of the opening instrumental passages, its function being to wipe the outer world from the slate of the
mind. They were comparatively emotionless and quite
pertinent. In the later Weimar cantatas those opening

[1] Eng. transl., Novello and Breitkopf editions.
[2] Eng. transl. Breitkopf edition.
[3] Eng. transl. Oxford University Press and Breitkopf editions.

bars grew and grew—being styled respectively, in the three cantatas just mentioned, Sinfonia, Overture, and Concerto—until they accept the name of the most insolent of musical forms, the concert-piece in which musical acrobats of the highest skill have always loved to disport themselves.

Such degree of impertinence was not easily touched by Bach. The Sinfonia of *Ich hatte viel Bekümmerniss* is at least modest in the matter of length. It accepts the Italian principle of the greater importance of a solo part, but it holds contact with the polyphonic spirit by offering *two* soloists playing in imitative form. It accepts the Italian principle of thematic decorativeness instead of the German principle of melodic expressiveness, but it preserves the living spirit of music by giving expressional value to the figuration. Hearing an Italian piece of that time, attention would be concentrated chiefly on the skill of the performers. Great technical skill is needed properly to bring out the beauty of the Bach phrases, but their emotional atmosphere is real enough to make one forget the skill of the performers in the greater wonder of the music. And there is a definitely dramatic effect in the chords and pauses of the final bars, and in the strange little figure which unexpectedly seems to cut off the music a bar before it is ended.

Is that little upward arpeggio a gentle sigh at the end of the melancholy? Or should it have a rougher interpretation, and suggest something of the impatient labour which Bach must have experienced in the making of the piece? For with all its beauties of detail, the cantata lacks dramatic continuity. It seems to have been put together from odds and ends which the composer had by him, rather than composed as a fairly schemed work from beginning to end. And the music chosen for the first chorus being entirely unsuitable for the words Bach seems to have made the introductory piece to give what the chorus could not give. But neither is there a clear message in the Sinfonia. Expressive though its phrases are, they do not reach the full and significant beauty of German melody.

Melody is supposed to be the chief, and indeed the only, considerable feature of Italian music. That is nonsense. Throughout the Christian era the Italian idea of melody has been superficial. Even the folk songs of the Italians have not the strength of character we find in the folk music of other Southern peoples, the Greeks and Spaniards. Indeed we may probably go a good deal further and say that from the pseudo-Greek art of Imperial Rome to the feeble flutings of Bellini and the verbose inflammation of d'Annunzio the indigenous Italians have shown a strange incapacity for noble creative art. It was in those parts of Italy which were settled by German tribes, that art of the noblest kind has arisen. Giotto and Dante were born in districts which were so settled.

The natural melody of Italy seems to have been so poor that its most representative composers have sought to disguise its shame with a florid and futile decoration of arabeskes; and that was the kind of music which evidently appealed to the ducal circle at Weimar. That is the kind of art which Bach is supposed to have imitated in the introduction to the *Bekümmerniss* cantata! Handel was at the same time copying the foolish art with more success, and losing something of his natural power in the effort. Bach in imitating the external appearance of the art filled it, as we have already seen, with whatever of music it could be made to hold; and though he was not allowed to make melody the basis of the whole structure he placed under the two solo parts a logically moving bass, and gave to it all a harmonic variety which must have seemed a little bewildering to the poor souls who were quite content with the Italian poverty of chord.

As already stated, the first chorus is a strange thing in which words and music seem almost opposed. Having expressed what he could of 'heart's affliction' in the complainings of the Sinfonia, Bach seems in the chorus almost wholly intent on making a music which will regain for him a sense of self-respect as a polyphonic artist. Instead of 'my heart was sad and sorrowful' a more fitting text would be 'I will not write that feeble stuff,' and then the musical quality of the chorus would sound right enough. The whole piece is strong in feeling, and the old communal principle of polyphony asserted with an onrush as of power which has been temporarily dammed up.

We can see that it cost Bach nothing but a wasteful restraint to make music in the Italian style. Whatever of lack of ease is shown in these cantatas is due, not to unskilfulness in doing an easy thing, but to a feeling as of musical suffocation because he was giving out so much less than he had to give, while the lack of dramatic values must have caused him almost to despair.

Beginning in weak melancholy and following on with an indignant assertion of strength, the first part of the cantata is continued in a series of numbers which give no clear line of emotional experience such as we saw in the earlier works. It would seem as if the chief idea of the compiler of the text had been to present an arrangement of varied emotion such as concert-givers try to effect when arranging their programmes. Such doings were nothing to the purpose of Bach. He made good music, gave a more intense reality to the detail; but his very power in the latter regard sometimes threw the whole thing out of focus.

Realistic phraseology he maintained, and sometimes so strikingly that without a dramatic basis it seems impertinent. Instead of enforcing a dramatic scheme it becomes a detail of detached interest. In *Nach dir* the realistic suggestion of the scale passage was the exposure of truth in spite of surrounding wrong. In the *Beküm-merniss* aria which tells of salt tears and stormy billows it seems, at first glance, as if the quality of the music and the greater reality of the emotional experience were of less importance than the opportunity for realistic cleverness afforded by the idea of angry waters. In the earlier cantata the realism served a dramatic intention. In the later cantata the passage actually interferes un-duly with the general emotion prevailing in the aria, and has little or no relation to the work as a whole, though, as we shall see presently, it may have been something in the nature of a personal outcry.

More dramatic significance attaches to the second part of the *Bekümmerniss* cantata, by reason of Bach's self-revealing treatment of the duet.

Call to mind the duet in *Gottes Zeit* in which the weary Christian gladly accepted death as a good ex-change for life; and although the *Bekümmerniss* duet expresses a truer and more dramatic conception than anything in the first part, it indicates another step in Bach's mental retreat; and, as compared with the earlier duet, gives a more dubious view of the Christian faith itself. The convinced Christian spirit of the *Actus Tragi-cus* at once accepted Christ's word that Paradise was the natural goal, and gave expression to that acceptance in one of the people's songs. In the later work the faith is less sure. It is a troubled and bewildered soul

that struggles to believe, but hesitates and halts, for
some time refusing to take even Christ's own word:

> Soul: Ah Jesu, my peace!
>   Where art thou, my light?
> Jesus: O soul, I am with thee.
> Soul: With me? Here is sheer night.

The soul cries for power to believe. The way continues
hard. In the music which follows faith is all but rejected. Jesus is even accused of hating the soul!

All this, interpreted in the light of any conceivable
shade of orthodoxy, is sheer nonsense. But when we
understand that Bach was revealing something of his
own position, which involved a kind of apostasy, a real
light is thrown upon the strange piece. It at once reminds us of the art-work of another great master who
also concealed, and all but renounced his faith, that he
might secure his career as creative artist. The stern and
terrible Christ-figure in Michael Angelo's 'Last Judgment' almost exactly pictures the soul's idea of Christ
in this music of Bach.

Bach was not only half repudiating the faith which
was natural to his inmost being; he was also rejecting
the traditional art which was the only means he had of
expressing his true belief. In the earlier duet we found
the chorale; in the later duet the people's song has no
place.

It is true that some degree of peace is eventually
reached by the trembling soul. Orthodoxy itself insisted

on that. But the long section of mistrust completely overweighs the short happy section; and even in the latter no real confidence is stated in Christ's word—it is a prayer for the ability to believe rather than belief itself.

But when in the next number the soul is rebuked:

> The more we mourn about our loss
> The heavier becomes our cross.

and again:

> Think not when wrong and hate oppress thee
> It is thy God doth thee forsake.
> He in thy breast doth dwell to bless thee
> If thou in Him thy trust do make.

the composer breaks into the chorale as if he could no longer endure his new limitations.

For this reproach of his despair Bach completely deserts his awkwardly assumed Italianisms. He falls back on the song of the people and upon the polyphonic style which we must surely now recognize as associated in his mind with the earlier and communal interpretation of Christianity.

And in that connection, note the reminiscence of the earlier and more actual conception of Christian doctrine in the last but one of the lines just quoted. It sounds like a paraphrase of Blake's words: 'God only acts and is in existing beings or men.'

Bach's service with the Duke of Weimar involved a kind of apostasy. Not only in the matter of religious opinion; but in his efforts to win a livelihood by making a more superficial music, the composer was rejecting the point of view which he and all his ancestry had held. By that he seems to have been reduced almost to despair. He was lost in the mood of wan hope which in the Middle Ages was held to be the unforgiveable sin, because it undermined the will for effort and action, thus cutting at the roots of a better life in the future.

We shall find him sinking deeper yet; but I would like to emphasize that at this moment of his career when he was being 'devoured by billows' it is of much significance that, after going under, he regained his swimming power; and that less by any virtue of his own creative skill, than by means of the sane beauty of those who had evolved the popular tunes and the musical style of an earlier Christianity. The nature of the rebuke in the chorale-chorus is such that the inner drama of his own life is the more fully revealed. This outburst of unmistakeable drama in the middle of an undramatic sequence of devotional music, and in the course of his efforts to adapt himself to a lower will, is another piece of evidence for the main argument of this study. By means of the outburst even the wholly inartistic explosion in the tearful tenor aria of the first part is shown as a possible detail of the underlying drama; and that leads us to believe that when Bach used an obviously realistic phrase he was not only displaying a certain bent as an artist, but may also have been unconsciously drawing attention to some detail of the drama of his own life, as well as the greater drama which began in Syria nearly two thousand years ago, and is only now coming to its end.[1]

Following the chorale-chorus is an aria of happy relief in which Bach once more beats the Italians at their own game; and that is the real end of the cantata. The subsequent and comparatively conventional chorus is thoroughly Italian in spirit and form—pompous and redundant.

In his first choral effort for the duke Bach had done his best to please; but the innate truth of the man tore through the artificiality of the Italian vogue as, later on, Beethoven tore through the form of the Italian Sonata, and Wagner through the formalism of Italian opera. Artistic formulas imposed from without forced each composer to push towards a living expression, through the dull repetitive forms and the cheap ornamental fripperies which had their roots in the false, unhappy conditions of life which were established in Europe at the time of the Renaissance. Each discovered his own natural capacity to express details of reality by seeking a path back to the communal ideal. In each case it was the impulse to express realities which caused them first to give vitality to a foreign convention, and

---

[1] Professor Petrie in *The Revolutions of Civilisation* shows how the rise and fall of each great civilisation has taken about two thousand years.

then to destroy it. But in Bach's case, at the moment in his career we have now reached, he had not thoroughly come to grips with the foreign form because he had a much more expressive and flexible form in his mind—the traditional cantata form of the North German composers; and for the time being we see him, not seeking to destroy the false, but trying to come to terms with it. Hence the hesitancy of *Bekümmerniss* as compared with his earlier works.

Italian arias and choruses Bach could take in his stride; but Italian recitative originated in the rhythms and inflexions of a foreign tongue, in which tongue of course it must have had a certain validity. The difficulty of adapting such recitative to the German language will be understood when we remember the like problem with which Handel was faced in his English oratorios, and the false accents and inflexions which so frequently resulted.

Recitative functions in vocal works because there are often moments—especially in dramatic music—when the mood of the singer is not emotionally warmed to the degree where melody is natural and inevitable. Recitative is supposed to be near enough to speech to offer a suitable medium for any dull but inevitable links in the story, and near enough to music to prevent the snag which occurs when a singer changes his medium from song to speech.[1]

[1] Except in musical comedy, where the change is a part of the fun.

BACH, THE MASTER

Simple observation will make it clear that speech has a very wide, and the singing voice a comparatively narrow, compass. Feelings of surprise will carry the speaking voice to very high notes, while suffering will often find utterance in very low tones—high notes and low notes beyond the power of singers to sustain. So it seems that a musical form which is required to approximate to speech will, for one thing, have a more extended range of pitch than vocal forms which are essentially lyrical. In other words, if the greater part of a dramatic singer's role depends upon the middle octave of the singing voice, the recitative passages for that same voice will cover a considerably wider compass.

But an outstanding feature of Italian recitative is the comparative narrowness of its scale-compass. Even so good a German composer as Schütz had followed the Italians in that respect; and it is another proof of Bach's indifference to the Italian method that he referred even his technic to the actions of normal life, even when he was by way of assuming a foreign manner.

Recitative was apparently taken over by the Italians from the Roman ritual where its prime purpose had been the carrying of utterances through large spaces. The Gregorian tradition, like the music for Jewish and Moslem ritual, and apparently like the method employed by Greek actors in the fifth century B.C., had for its original purpose the carrying of utterances through large spaces. Extra and unnecessary notes were later on added to draw attention to important words, and even to express something of the feeling which accompanied the thought, as the colouring of illuminated manuscripts became a pictorial expression of the moods and meanings of the writing. A similar line was traced by the Italians from their dry recitative to their accompanied recitative, and by Bach when he passed from musical declamation to arioso.

As conditions of life enabled men to devote themselves to things of the human spirit (nearly always translated into terms of art and beauty) the narrow range of colour in the missal and the narrow range of tone in the musicalized speech grew into images and melodies, and the Christian world became aware of that climax of beauty which matured at Chartres and other places, grew richly ripe in Tuscany, then crystallized in Tudor literature, and finally melted out in the aerial art of music.

During the decline of good material conditions of life, the image ceased to have relation to the page, and melody grew more important than the feeling it conveyed. That is evidence in the Italian music of Bach's time—for Italians were always the quickest, as Germans were the slowest people to mature. So far as Bach's Italian contemporaries were concerned the final rot had already begun; and it is noteworthy that although he made glorified imitations of their more luxuriant musical forms, he practically ignored the basis of their dramatic vocal art—the dry recitative—and stuck to the natural melody of his own German speech. In his fidelity to that speech-melody he created a dramatic medium which anticipated the declamatory vocal music of Wagner.

Professor Dent in his study of Mozart's operas has some very interesting pages on Italian recitative, in which he finds validity if it is vocalised at the same rate as ordinary speech. That might serve in a small room; but as spaces grow larger speech must grow slower and more resonant with musical quality. We, like the Italians and, to a lesser degree, like Bach, have to consider the pace and fitness of musicalised speech in theatres and concert-rooms where a conversational speed is out of the question. It was for large spaces that the Italians developed their conventionalized monotony; for moderately large spaces Bach devised his realistic declamation.

Though the high notes of exasperation and the low notes of threat, for example, are beyond the normal range of vocal usage and could not be sustained in song, it is possible to give in musical notation something of their vocal outline and reality of feeling. That is what Bach does. For the Italians and for some of Bach's own German predecessors—Schütz, for example—the recitative is a mere sort of colour-decoration and tone-carrier for phrases which are not emotional enough to be worth setting to formal music, though they are needed if the thread of the story or thought is to be continuous.

The roots of Bach's recitative are in the hearts of German Christians, not in the conventions of an organized priesthood; for the Gregorian tradition was a voice of authority, pontifical and unemotional.

This early artistic decision and consistent adherence thereto are characteristic of Bach. His steadiness of style has been adduced as a sign that there is no real growth in his artistry from the earlier to the later cantatas: such growth as, for example, we find in the development of Beethoven's symphonies and Wagner's music-dramas. That is an unnecessary criticism, calculated to give a false impression of the greatest master of the three. So far as the external form of the cantatas was concerned there was no room or need for development. Bach had simply to use what texts he could, and give to them a true musical expression. The form was already perfect, in the same way that the Catholic Mass was a perfect art-form.

An artist who comes on the crest of a cultural wave has no need to develop his material; he has to fit his craftsmanship for the service and carry on. Once Bach had trained himself as craftsman his work was perfect, because he was serving something greater than a personal art. What seems like development in the works of Beethoven and Wagner was not development in the sense of moving their art towards some greater goal than is to be found in Bach; on the contrary, theirs were reactionary movements back towards Bach.

Behind the symphonies of Beethoven there lay the naive practice of Haydn and the perfect and wasted craftsmanship of Mozart. It took Beethoven but two attempts in the Mozartian symphony to know what he wanted to do in that form, and to realize that there was little worth doing. Life was outside that workshop; and Beethoven, like Bach, was the sort of man who must discover life at all costs. From the time of the Eroica Symphony Beethoven's was no mere artistic development, but a general mental growth during which the artist was thrusting his way into reality. And inevitably the thrust carried backward towards Bach.

The characteristics of the Mozartian symphony were prevailingly Italian. Homophonic style, Palladian balance, insignificant theme, and harmonic consonance were, as we have already seen, the outstanding feature of the Italian school. Beethoven set himself the task of winning back polyphonic power: he organized his movements as Bach had organized his fugues and the Gothic builders their cathedrals, not to fulfil a pre-decided form, but to express the fullness of their own inherent value; and that value was often based, not upon a fragment of theme, but upon a definite tune.

The great communal art of which Mozart had a glimpse in his declining days, and Beethoven fought for with all his power, was, in the time of Bach, still a

reality so far as music was concerned. Under such conditions a musician had only to be a faithful Christian
and a fine craftsman to be a noble artist. All Bach had
to decide was whether, having won his craft, he would
by its means serve a good or a bad cause, an important
or an affected cause, a German and popular or a foreign and snobbish cause.

So long as he could he served the good, important,
and popular cause. When a livelihood was not allowed
to him in that service he did such works as were demanded, and filled them with references, some clear,
some obscure, to the good cause—the cause considered
bad by Roman and Lutheran orthodoxies alike.

The master's engagement with Duke Ernst came
to an unpleasant end. No material benefit had been
won by Bach's attempts to disguise the nature and significance of his art. On the death of Capellmeister
Drese the appointment was given, not to the genius
available, but to the dead man's son, a musical nonentity.

A little later Bach was offered a capellmeister's position in the service of Count Leopold of Anhalt Cöthen.
On the composer's request for release from the Weimar
engagement, the unspeakable duke ordered him to be
arrested!

After keeping his menial in detention for about a
month the duke discovered that arbitrary hangings,
drawings, and quarterings were unfortunately no longer
in fashion; so he released the musician from a position

which must, in any case, have carried with it something of the feeling of imprisonment, even from the beginning. Even if Bach had been in a less unhappy condition than that member of his family who had not been allowed to visit his children, what sort of duty was it for a man when he could not give true expression to his own religious thoughts, nor even to his own musical genius!

The day had not yet come when, religion being dead, music had no purpose but that of putting men's thoughts to sleep.

Chapter Eight

THE GILDED CAGE

A DEFINITE feeling of relief pervades the music which Bach wrote at Cöthen, where his abilities seem to have been fairly recognized by the Prince, who gave proofs of real musical taste and friendship.

Imagine the expansion of the composer's thoughts and feelings when he began to realize the change he was enjoying. His musical resources were rather limited. Instead of a chorus there was at his disposal only a couple of solo voices, and for instruments a small chamber orchestra. But he was not the first musician, nor the last, to experience the peculiar pleasure there is in devoting the whole of his power to the development and, so far as attainable, the perfecting, of intimate forms with comparatively small means.

As a period in his creative life the time at Cöthen was less important than the years which were yet to follow. The music made then naturally contributed little to the expression and stimulation of the greater life of his time; but for sheer growth of musical artistry it was of much importance. The exquisite things which flowed from the master in the seclusion of chamber-form were preceded by a vocal work, poor enough in word and purpose, but radiant with a spirit of thankfulness consequent upon his release from a more degrading footmanship.

A Birthday Serenade exists in which he seems to have expressed his first joy in serving a master who was at the same time a music-lover. The words are feeble and servile enough.

The new service was still the narrow service of a private master, though it had cast off its musical repression and resentment. A decent dress had taken the place of a comic livery. Some cause an artist must serve. If, instead of the welfare of a community, he must answer the will and pleasure of another man, it is at least good when the person served realizes the honour he is receiving. Prince Leopold seems to have known; and if Bach was still in some ways caged, the cage was gilded, and his mind left free.

No church music was required of him there, though two or three cantatas date from that period. But before considering the chamber works it will be well to examine the one or two vocal works for whatever of light their words and treatment throw upon Bach's mental life during that time.

Of the few sacred cantatas written at Cöthen one is easily available in an English translation, and reveals the greater public spirit which still formed the background of Bach's mind.

The words of the opening duet of *Du wahrer Gott* run, in the translation of Thorne and Daisley:

> Thou very God and David's son!
> Out of the dim recess ere time had yet begun,
> My heart's distress, my body's agony,
> Thou knewest and dost know. O, pity me;
> And let Thy wonder-working hand,
> That can alone hell's power command,
> On me a saving health bestow.

Thus far the sentiment seems personal and private enough; but in the recitative which follows the composer does a curious and significant thing. The words of the recitative are:

Ah, go not Thou far from me, Thou Saviour of mankind,
To cheer the wearied, the feeble folk, and not the strong,
Hast Thou appeared.
Therefore Thy mighty power shall be with mine combined.
Though dim they are, mine eyes confess thee.
Upon this path, where to distress me
The world doth bid me tread,
I'll cleave to Thee, and leave to Thee
No choice unless Thou bless me.

Here again we have a libretto by an 'unknown' poet, who can scarcely have been other than Bach himself.

Notice the reversion to the earlier and truer conception of Christianity in the second and third lines; notice the association of godlike and human power in the fourth; notice the personal tone of the remaining lines;

and consider the meaning of it all in the light of Bach's apparent weakening of faith at Weimar. Notice how the final lines declare that, though the musician felt his outward career was more or less committed to the kind of service he was engaged upon, he intended to let go nothing of his inmost convictions.

In view of that piece of self-revelation the manner of its musical setting is the more remarkable. No ordinary recitative would do. An important thing had to be asserted for which only the music of the people would serve; and so he came upon a new and interesting form—a folk-music in strict time with a running commentary of verse.

Here again is witness to show that Bach looked on the chorale as the original and most vital expression of popular and essential Christianity—the religion which was to have saved the weak and feeble, and *not* the strong. His use of the chorale is again unmistakeable. He had used it regularly when he was in the public service. He had ceased to use it during his period of court service, though this cantata was written at Cöthen it was intended to pave the way for his return to a public career. He did not use the chorale for the personal mood of the previous number; but for more direct ideas he found it necessary, although couched in the unlikely form of a recitative.

At Cöthen he was apparently as happy as an artist could be whose full powers had no means of expression,

BACH PLAYING FOR FREDERICK THE GREAT

whose real thoughts no natural outlet in his art; but this cantata was composed in the later days when he was hoping for an appointment elsewhere. The matter is introduced at this point in our study that we have some indication of the ideas which haunted the master's thoughts during his days of secluded ease.

What peace of mind means to a scientist, a scholar, or an artist can scarcely be understood by men and women who find the chief expression of their lives in action and social intercourse. The unusual and inconvenient combination of characteristics in men who must live apart from the world if they are to do their work properly, and must at the same time belong to the world in an extra special degree if their work when done is to function fairly, makes life a hard thing for them. They have a need for personal solitude, and at the same time a need to give public service. They often have a positive distaste for action, and at the same time are engaged in the production of works which are ineffective until they are brought into activity.

Onlookers have often regarded such lives as devoted to idleness and self-enjoyment, whereas they are generally lives of hard and continuous struggle. And I think it will be found that only those artists who have been able to extract from the world a certain measure of the conditions indicated have ever properly made good. Schubert had privacy for his personal work, but never a fair opportunity for the public to influence him. Berlioz and Liszt well understood the public service but had not enough solitude in which to incubate their ideas. Bach, Mozart, Beethoven, Mendelssohn, Wagner, and others at one time or other in their lives found opportunity for the unfolding of both parts of their characters.

Bach got his time of mental ease at the age of thirty-two and proceeded to write a series of intimate and beautiful works which has ennobled even the annals of Teuton aristocracy. During the first two or three years at Cöthen he seems to have composed little. Besides travelling with his prince he was allowed to make journeys on his own account for the sake of his art. But in 1720 his wife died; and then he seems to have devoted himself to the making of his chamber works.

A few months before Maria Barbara's death there were musical signs of Bach's interest in the members of his family. Discovering that his son Wilhelm Friedemann had considerable gifts, he composed various little teaching pieces; and that act of fatherhood led him to explore certain aspects of music which hitherto had been regarded as outside the range of practical art.

He started with the idea of making the beginner familiar with the feeling of his fingers in all likely keys, and with the polyphonic principle of uniting two or three voices in a single thematic development. The pieces were no mere exercises. Bach could no more dissociate the activity of the fingers from the activity of the brain, than he could dissociate the service of art from the service of the highest ideas that he knew. So what were intended as exercises became exquisite little works of art.

As we play the Inventions and Symphonies we find them growing in richness and loveliness. This series of pieces is not only useful for study and delightful to hear; it is a landmark in the history of musical development. In the making of the pieces the composer was led from the initial purpose of giving finger facility in various keys to the exploration of forbidden key paths. The adventure must have been rather like that of those artists who passed from a narrow range of colour to the beauties of subtle blendings.

Although the key signatures of the Inventions and Symphonies go no further than four sharps and flats, the modulations through which they pass touch such extreme keys as G sharp minor and E flat minor; so they prepare the way for the Forty-Eight Preludes and Fugues wherein the master asserted the musician's right to the use of a full palette.

Starting with the idea of helping his little son on a difficult journey through as many sharps and flats as he would be likely to encounter, Bach added to the number of such difficulties, taking his stand by those progressives who aimed at a more equal tuning of keyed instruments.

The French Suites also were the outcome of Wilhelm

Friedemann's studies, while some of the pieces then composed found their final place in the well tempered Clavichord itself.

We are sometimes inclined to marvel at the difficulty of a few of those pieces, intended as they were for the use of a boy of ten years. Indeed we may even be surprised at the considerable technic required for other and more advanced works by Bach. Such technic was apparently nothing out of the way. If anything there had been before Bach's time a decline in the general performing ability of musicians. That seems clear if we compare the most difficult of the Bach works for keyed instrument with some of Bull's compositions in the Fitzwilliam Virginals Book. It was a decline comparable in some ways with the decline in polyphonic choral music between the thirteenth and seventeenth centuries.

The Elizabethan madrigal composers were the last wave but one, while Bach and Handel were the last wave, of a musical tide which had reached its great and popular crest in the thirteenth century. The restricted public appeal of the later composers was associated, it is true, with a more consummate skill and a more subtle emotional fragrance; but the later men had centuries of traditional skill behind them, as well as centuries of public artistic spirit, and their music was a pledge of their various attempts to recapture a spirit which earlier on had been the spirit of all Christendom.

Only a small and select audience of what we should

now call county people had culture enough to answer to the musical appeal of the Elizabethans; and the music suffered accordingly in depth of human feeling and breadth of human sympathy. Having exhausted their vocal imaginations in association with subtle ideas and classical allusions, the madrigalians fell back on folk-tune variations for harpsichord and virginals for sheer need of their musical natures, half-starved as they must have been by the affected taste of their patrons.

We have only to open a book of madrigals at random to meet with evidence of such over-refinement of mood:

> Alas, quoth I, what meaneth this demeanour?
> So fair a dame to be so full of sorrow:
> No wonder, quoth a nymph, she wanteth pleasure;
> Her tears and sighs ne cease from eve to morrow:
> This lady rich is of the gifts of beauty,
> But unto her are gifts of fortune dainty.[1]

And even as the too delicate mood of the madrigal had degenerated from the lusty public joy of 'Sumer is icumen in' and its like, so the affections of Elizabethan patronage soon reduced the hearty associations of the folk-song variations to displays of extreme technical difficulty such as we find in the pieces of Bull.

The bravado of Bull's as compared with the force of Bach's less extravagant technic is one proof that the value of craftsmanship is relative. A certain amount of skill is necessary for the expression of ideas; if an ex-

[1] From Byrd's *Songs of Sundry Natures,* 1589.

travagant and obvious technic is used it is because there
is an absence of ideas.

What the winning of such an executive ability as
Bull's meant of time and labour is best left to the
imagination; and Bull was not alone, even though the
most extreme of that time. Technical ability in Bach's
young days was certainly less extravagant, as witness the
Bible Sonatas of Kuhnau; but there must have been
in existence, and known to the Bach family, many keyboard pieces of great difficulty. So the Clavier-büchlein
which to us seems rather a book for intermediate pupils,
was for young Wilhelm Friedemann an elementary
book of studies. Its main purpose was certainly not that
of dazzling an audience with an exhibition of finger
tricks, but a means of acquiring such skill as would
enable a keyboard instrument to give a definite idea of
the many-melodied style from which all the best music
known to Bach had sprung—a style which was taken
over by the organ and piano tribe partly because it was
the style of the great tradition, partly because (as we
have seen in the case of the organ) the decline in the
concerted or communal practice of music had made it
necessary to transfer the whole art and craft to those
unsatisfactory instruments—instruments which were
conveniently adapted to the change from communal to
solo practice, but were entirely unsuited for the finer
and fuller revelations of polyphony.

After Bach's death the disintegration of polyphony

was rapid. Mozart stemmed it, but added nothing that was not known to Bach. Beethoven could not recapture it, though he tried hard enough, rightly feeling that only in a polyphonic music could the ordered spirit of Freedom find a natural voice. A homophonic style could well serve as background for the narrower thoughts more fitting for the medium of a soloist, but it could only express the multitude as a mob—never as a vital organism of many individuals.

Consequently, in most of Bach's pieces for solo instruments there is a paradox which can only be resolved by transferring them to their rightful medium—the concerted group, from string duet to full orchestra—the more especially as we live in a time when the organ is disappearing as an instrument of art, and continuing chiefly as a museum specimen in church or a diseased debauchee in the cinema.

The fact that so many short clavier pieces made at various times by Bach should afterwards have been collected by him as Prelude and Fugue, Invention and Symphony, Suite, and so on, according to their key-relationship, has a significance which is often overlooked in these days when the sense of key is in danger of dissolution.

Both melody and harmony have a mathematical basis, though they were actually developed by process of experiment. By what steps those musical elements reached their final form in European music there is no room here to trace; but this much is certain and must be emphasized, that the earlier and modal forms of melody, and the earlier and consonantal forms of harmony, are characteristic of an art which has not even begun to reach its climax.

Primitive harmony may be best studied in its extempore forms at social gatherings or during the march of soldiers, and not in its earlier scholastic forms. The outstanding characteristic of primitive harmony is its lack of dissonance.

Primitive melody may be heard in the songs of birds and babies. Before folk-music could be properly recorded it was necessary to introduce the gramophone, because the intermediate scale sounds of the folk-singers could not be properly shown in conventional notation. Later forms of melody have a clearer definition of scale, at first without, and then with, a feeling for a keynote. Finally, what we call the major scale dominated all the best music of Europe. That progress from vagueness to definition of pitch and note relationship is a good example of the truth contained in Blake's pregnant sentences: 'Nature has no outline, but Imagination has. Nature has no tune, but Imagination has.'

The degenerate tendency of our own day to renounce what was so hardly won has also been well expressed by the same author:

> These are the Idiot's chiefest arts,
> To blend and not define the parts.

To make out the parts is the wise man's aim,
But to loose them the fool makes his foolish aim.

Nor must the loose structure of Blake's own verse cause us to be careless of the truths it contains.

In Bach's time the slight differences between Ionian, Lydian, and Mixolydian modes on the one hand, and on the other between the Dorian, Phrygian, and Aeolian modes, had coalesced as major and minor scales respectively. In that process the minor scale became nearly approximated to the major by the eventual use of the major sixth (existing only in Dorian) and the major seventh (existing in no mode with a minor third). Bach clinched the matter by drawing up his shorter pieces as associated groups of compositions in major or minor keys; and he still further emphasized the greater importance of the major by using in his minor pieces that final major chord which only can give a proper sense of complete settlement.

We have only to compare Suites by earlier composers with the Suites of Bach to realize the steady growth of the key-sense.

The idea of a keynote was practically established by the time of the Fitzwilliam Virginals book in spite of which many of those pieces have but an indifferent sense of key. They wander to and fro in the various modes, at one moment yielding to a healthy instinct for the sharpened seventh, and immediately afterwards basing a whole passage on the flattened seventh—a habit probably derived from the drones of bagpipes. Examples are many, but at random I may instance Byrd's Variations on Sellenger's Round and on Tregian's Ground.

By Purcell's time so definite an interposition of harmony on the flattened seventh had become impossible, though melodic juxtapositions of the sharpened and flattened sixth or seventh were possible as in the Prelude to the English master's Suite in G minor. To compensate for the loss of harmonic variety a timid feeling for modulation began to develop; and in that same Prelude the composer passed into D minor, besides hinting at C minor and B flat major.

Couperin went a step further. Thus in his B minor Suite commencing with the piece called *La Raphaele* he modulated momentarily into A major, E minor, D major, and F sharp minor. His full closes in those keys are more defined than Purcell's: that makes it clear that for Couperin the main key seemed more definitely established, so that he could move from it without losing a sense of the home key. But it is to be noticed that whenever Couperin settled upon the dominant cadence as a kind of half-way resting place, he insisted by means of a flattened sub-dominant that he had not finally left the chief key of the piece.

When Bach accepted the principle of that halfway house he boldly modulated into another key, and announced the fact by means of a sharpened seventh. Moreover, Bach modulated more freely than did Couperin. In his French Suite in B minor (to choose for an example a work in the same key) we find modulations into D major, F sharp minor, F sharp major, E minor and A major—one more key change than in the Couperin. And whereas Couperin's most sustained modulation lasts for sixteen beats, in the Gigue movement of the Bach Suite there is a passage in D major which endures for thirty-three beats, besides passages well-sustained in other keys. One more point: after each key-departure Couperin reverted to the chief key, but Bach established his chief key so well that he felt free to roam throughout two or three byways of key-tonality before returning to his main road.

Key sense had to be established to save musical art from the similarities and vagueness of the modes. A danger of monotony was then observed, but was avoided by free modulation into related keys. The range of modulation was extended after Bach's time, until a moment came when it defeated its own end. Too frequent and over-restless modulation becomes as vague and monotonous as was the early modal music. Music which attempts freedom from key-restriction attains that freedom with a result not altogether intended by its advocates, by asserting a freedom from any sort of coherent appeal. It was the kind of freedom which Prospero allowed to Ariel only when his work was completed. 'To the *elements* be thou free!' but as Blake said, 'Nature has no outline.'

In much music that is being made to-day there is no intelligible thought because the elements of music have been freed from the discipline (among other things) of the key sense which was so carefully evolved in the rise of our civilization and crown by the genius of Bach.

A composer like Debussy added something to music by reviving modal subtleties which had been dropped and forgotten in the heyday of key-recognition. That hey-day was subsequent to the time of Bach who wrote many a piece in which the peculiar flavour of the modes was preserved.

When we return to the art of Bach after a long dose of music without definite key-relationship, the older and clearer ways of musical thought seem like a welcome anchorage after a very busy, very dull, and almost useless voyage. But whereas for us modulation is a return home after a strange and stormy journey, for Bach it was a great adventure which ended in the colonization of new countries.

One of the lesser details of his exploration was the special advantage offered by remote keys to performers on keyboard instruments. Like Chopin later on, Bach recognized that certain keys hitherto unused were peculiarly suited to the lie of the hand upon the fingerboard. We have only to examine those pieces in The Forty-eight Preludes and Fugues which are written in several sharps or flats to realize that the form of the hands in those keys actually indicated to the master

many a passage of fresh and effective music. The rapid
fingerwork in the Preludes in E flat minor and F sharp
major in the First Book, and the Preludes in C sharp
major, F sharp major, and G sharp minor in the Second
Book, offer examples of delicate ideas possible just because of the position of the hand in those particular keys.
Such influence shows to a lesser extent in the Fugues,
because in them the master is limited by his greater consideration for the polyphonic scheme; but even in some
of the Fugues a similar tendency is to be noticed—in the
F sharp major Fugue of the first set, and the Fugues
in C sharp major and B major in the second set.

Emotional suggestions as arising from key are less
marked; but, in the two preludes and the two fugues
in A flat there seems to be a quality which Bach did not
reach in any other key, at any rate among the pieces
for clavier. This aspect of key values, however, cannot
be pressed. Bach wrote tenderly and even pianistically
in other keys than A flat; but (and especially recalling
Chopin's fondness for that same key in relation to that
same feeling) it would seem that for all composers certain keys are associated with certain moods. Is not the
very word mood but another form of the word mode?
It seems not unlikely therefore, that the limpid beauty
of Bach's pieces in C sharp and F sharp major, the
gentle loveliness of those in A flat, and the strange poig-
nancy of those in F minor and G sharp minor, derive to
some extent from the fact that the master in extending

his key range had discovered wider possibilities for his growing expressive powers.

He is said to have written the First Book of the Forty-eight during an enforced absence from home and from regular musical activity while he accompanied his master on a visit.

A few of the pieces apparently existed before that time, but the majority seem to have been written consecutively in fulfilment of his key explorations. That they may also contain some expression of the repressed part of his mind seems likely. The Fugue in F sharp minor contains an outstanding passage which reminds us of the figure Bach used to express 'a weary dragging walk' in connection with the idea of burial. The Fugues in G minor and G sharp minor, have a curious drooping phrase, while the Fugue in B minor must be named with the most poignant of the master's music. But the chief and almost continuous mood of this part of The Forty-eight is of cheerfulness in all its phases, from the calm assurance of the Fugue in C major to the exuberant joy of the Fugue in G major. These are tokens of the happier mental life Bach was enjoying.

Reference has already been made to the inability of keyboard instruments properly to render the multitudinous life of polyphonic music. That would seem to apply in even greater strength to the Sonatas for solo violin and violoncello; but there is less difference than might be expected in that regard, because a difference in the shapes of bridge and bow in Bach's time made polyphony almost as possible on bowed instruments as on those with keyboard. Whatever is unsatisfactory in those works is due less to technical difficulties than to the obvious paradox of a single performer pretending to give real and separate life to several voices. On the technical side the works for solo strings were as perfect and amazing as those for organ or for those of the clavier family. In a certain sense the string works are even more important; for, as Schweitzer pointed out, Bach was a fiddler before he was an organist, and his musical idiom is more frequently derived from fiddle phrasing. Because of that the solo sonatas are in a certain sense key works.

The effect of the flatter bridge and differently constructed bow seems to have resulted in a soft quality of tone, a tone more like that of the old viols than of the modern violin. From that it is clear that the solo sonatas are not solos in the modern sense of the word —not solos for the display of virtuosity, though their difficulties are in some ways greater than the more vulgar and obvious difficulties of later virtuoso music: not solos for the concert platform, but examples of chamber-music in solo form, and intended for a gathering of friends rather than for public performance.

The wonderful sonatas for clavier and violin are better known, and more truly answer to the polyphonic demands of Bach's genius. They must be understood not as duets but as trios, two voices sounding on the clavier and the third on the violin. They certainly contain a few passages in which each instrument predominates and develops something of its own idiosyncracies: for examples, the violin arpeggios in the last movement of the A major, and the decorative figures in the cembalo part of the F minor Sonatas; but even a cursory glance at these pieces reveals the fact that there are three continuous parts of an importance that is practically equal.

Verbal analysis of instrumental music is a vain thing, and I do not propose to weary the reader with descriptions of works which must be meaningless unless the works are heard, and unnecessary when a hearing is possible. All we can do here is to draw attention to the deeper and sadder moods which again began to pre-occupy the master's mind; and to a more obvious relationship between some movements in these works and the greater world which pursued Bach even into his retreat at Cöthen.

Schweitzer has called attention to the likeness between the Siciliano of the C minor Sonata and one of the most sorrowful arias in the *St. Matthew* Passion. There are two other details which suggest some dramatic intention behind the purely musical expression of the pieces. One is the first movement of the F minor Sonata with its incessant repetition of phrase in the clavier part and the long drawn commentary in the violin part; the other is the complete exclusion of the violin in the third movement of the G major Sonata.

Some light is thrown on the dramatic meaning of the F minor movement when we learn that the chief subject belongs also to a motet with the words, 'Come, Jesu, come, for I am weary.' For the exclusion of the violin in the other movement we have no clue or reason. It may have been accidental; but an accident so singular in the case of a great craftsman like Bach inclines one to imagine dramatic intention there also.

It has been suggested with some show of likelihood that the more unhappy movements in these works may have been in some way connected with the death of Bach's first wife, which happened at Cöthen. But the words associated with the vocal forms of the above pieces refer rather to the less personal problems which possessed every important work of the master throughout his life.

From the Sonatas to the Violin Concertos is a step from the intimate family relations of chamber music into that communal art wherein Bach's genius found fullest expression. At first thought such a step seems surprising. Concertos for soloist and orchestra are in our days the musical application of an evil principle wherein one individual is pedestalled and disports himself more or less amazingly, while the orchestral crowd of lost individualities exists only to further the glory of, and give an occasional rest to, the soloist. The evil of that kind of concerto is not to be found in any work of Bach.

Even Bach's concertos with a single soloist preserve modesty in the chief part and much variety and interest in the tutti sections. We can hear the composer in these works explaining that though his prince is a very good fiddler it takes more than a single performer to give a good concert; while the rest of the entertainment is likely to be all the more amusing if every part is made as interesting as possible. With such a point of view it was certain that the concerto form would be transformed from the mere exhibition of harmless agility such as Corelli and Vivaldi had made it, and would become a vehicle for the statement of real musical problems and the expression of real musical feeling. And we must remember that the very title had a different connotation for Bach than it has to-day.

We, with modern concerto-monstrosities from Liszt to Prokoviev and Stravinsky in our minds, find it harder than Bach did to divorce the form from solo-display. Notwithstanding the dangerous turn given to the concerto by its Italian creators, Bach kept it almost entirely to that original sense which made it a series of pieces suitable for a meeting of friends—a concerted effort in terms of music. Already at Weimar he had written 'concertos' as introductory instrumental pieces to church cantatas; and though the admission of so long and barely relevant a movement was significant of a definite backsliding in the service of a religious cause, the master did not allow such introductions to degenerate into show pieces for soloists.

The essential relation between the solo and tutti parts of a Bach Concerto is very like the essential relation between so-called 'great men' and the ordinary people of their time.

In the work of such men as Giotto, Shakespeare, Oliver Cromwell, and Bach himself, there were clearly two main factors: the first, made up of the traditions they inherited, and the habits and ideas of the general public which had arisen in those traditions; the second, whatever was singular in themselves.

It is unnecessary to stress the obvious differences between Giotto and his fellow shepherds, Shakespeare and his brother butchers, Cromwell and his Puritan associates, Bach and his Protestant comrades; but it may not be unwise to recall the fact that the art of Giotto could only have taken the general form it did in the Christian communes of northern Italy, and Giotto was but one of a group of great painters so alike in their genius that there is some doubt regarding the authorship of certain works ascribed to him; that the art of Shakespeare could only have taken its florid, snobbish, and lusciously poetical form in the service of a comparatively small and leisurely class, and Shakespeare was but one of a great group of playwrights so like in their blatant methods that Shakespeare stands

out from his fellows chiefly because of his willingness
to express the commoner, sweeter, and less arrogant
aspects of life as well as the mock heroics which he
shared with the others; that Cromwell was but one,
and by no means the noblest, of a group of men in
revolt against an intolerable political system which was
reducing the whole people to beggary; that Bach himself, as we have already seen, derived most of his essential 'greatness' from his use of the traditional polyphonic
methods, and his acceptance of the people's song as
the basis of his work. He came at a time when all the
hardest upbuilding work had been done, and stands
out in our view chiefly because he was truer to the real
significance of his religion than the majority of artists
of his time, truer to his traditions, religious and musical, than even Handel.

None knew better than Bach himself that the only
part of his art which he might claim as his own was
due to the personal industry and honesty of his workmanship—and even that we now know to have been
the result of tradition, birth, habit, and circumstance.

What remains of personal 'rights' and individual art
is indeed little. That Bach sensed the actual relationship between an outstanding individuality and the mass
from which it sprang and to which it belongs, is nowhere
more clear than in his concertos. It is not merely that
the orchestral masses are full of living detail; it is
not merely that some of the orchestral sections are as

important and beautiful as the solo-parts; it is also that the solo-parts nearly always carry a greater responsibility equal to their more apparent importance. The solo parts in the violin concertos are not the spoiled pets, but the actual leaders, of the whole work. The solo parts in the clavier concertos are not autocrats of the music-making, but ministers who carry on the continuo bass throughout, and bear a continuous responsibility of the whole thing; and in this connection it is well to recall the fact that the very word lead is cognate with load, and a leader one who bears the load. More than that even! We have recalled examples of 'great men' and noticed that they seem to have come, not as isolated phenomena, but as members of a general movement in life. That has its parallel in the concertos of Bach; for while he wrote nine for solo instruments associated with orchestra, he wrote no fewer than twelve with more than one solo part, and two without solos of any kind.

This intuitive sense of a natural human relation between leaders and masses inevitably results in works of art as much nobler than the concerto form of to-day, as a community wherein the leaders are also the load-bearers is bound to be nobler than a community in which the leaders are loafers, pilferers, and showmen. A slight degree of vanity may be permitted to a leader—the sort of vanity Bach allows his soloists—the pride of carrying out an important task well, the pleasure in leading a number of people into a world of wider experience and greater beauty—even an occasional vanity in the exposition of exceptional craftsmanship; but never the vanity of feeling idly superior, the vicious vanity which really ends leadership, and degrades concerted music.

We need not elaborate that final decadence of the 'great man' idea, in which real leadership having been lost in vain postures and impostures, we reach the relationship of pushers and pushed, for though we often see examples of that on our own concert platforms there is of course no such parallel in the concertos of Bach.

Because of the vital principles which were continually stirring in the mind of Bach, he could not for ever be content with such means of expression as was afforded by even the highest forms of instrumental music. It could relieve his emotional spirit, but it could not offer a proper means of asserting those principles in the common world. It must often have seemed to the master that at Cöthen he was cut off from the most important part of life. Without the originating stimulus of the real outer world his genius was, as it were, singing in a cage—singing there as a lark would sing, well cared for, loved perhaps, but existing without a share in the material and essential processes of life.

There are signs of unuttered longing in some of those very instrumental works. In some of the violin concertos as well as in the sonatas there are thematic reflections of the deeper moods which he exposed more fully and directly in vocal works. The slow movement of the Violin Concerto in E major has a meaning which is more fully delivered in the first alto aria of the St John Passion; while there is almost as definite a relationship between the finale of the same concerto and the seventh number of the Passion.

He was probably already engaged on that beautiful work, and reflected in his instrumental pieces something of its moods. In spite of material ease and musical freedom he was not happy, was not satisfied with that narrow parasitic life, was already looking out for an opportunity of taking part once again in the common life where only could his genius get proper stimulation, even if no adequate recognition.

So it happened that the crowning achievement of Bach's genius at Cöthen was not an instrumental work, but a composition which reaches out from the vague and inner world whence music issues towards the most vital form of Christian belief. The St John Passion was for Bach himself, not an oratorio, but an expression of his faith in the most vivid and dramatic form available. It was a true descendant of the mystery plays of the Middle Ages.

That Bach should have composed such a work as this Passion—a work which must have demanded all likely musical resources of the large city—while yet he was limited by the narrow life and meagre material of a private chamber musician, gives some idea of his feelings in that caged condition.

It has been suggested that the work was commissioned by the Leipsic Town Council during the Cöthen period. That seems very doubtful in view of their inability to perform such a piece in the existing state of their choir, the boys especially having run wild under a slack and poverty-stricken regime. Nor, if Bach had actually been asked for such a work by them, would they have subsequently required of him the much smaller evidence of his powers (and suitability for the post of Cantor!) in the form of a church cantata.

Again, it seems unlikely that the Leipsic Council would have commissioned an important work from Bach, and performed it in 1723 before his appointment, the appointment itself being indeed in the air though by no means decided on, and almost certainly give such a performance as would have made the composer less likely to have accepted the appointment afterwards—to say nothing of the fact that Bach could scarcely have scrambled through the composition of the work in time enough for its production on Good Friday of that year.

The St John Passion may very well have been first performed at Leipsic after Bach had settled there; but its composition is more likely to have originated in a natural creative impulse. His work at Cöthen occupied neither all his time nor all his mind; indeed, the deeper wells of his character were scarcely drawn upon in Prince Leopold's service. The kindness of a cultured master was no real stimulus in default of the present emotions of the outer world.

The text was based on a well known Passion poem which was set by several composers of that time, including Handel. Bach reshaped the libretto, added to it and modified it to a large extent; so it has been suggested that he received the help of some 'delicate unknown poet.' But he was himself quite equal to the occasion. If my earlier suggestions are correct he had already supplied himself with better texts than were otherwise available. In any case, we know that when the occasion demanded a setting by him of some official poet's words, he was by no means diffident about alterations and interpolations to suit his own more vital conceptions.

Chambers tells us that 'the dramatic tendencies of Christian worship declared themselves at a very early period. At least from the fourth century the central and most solemn rite in that worship was the Mass, an essentially dramatic commemoration of one of the most critical moments in the life of the Founder.'[1]

Passion plays had their rise in the twelfth century, at that significant moment of Christian civilization when the tide of popular development was first dangerously

[1] *The Medieval Stage*, II, 3, by E. K. Chambers.

threatened, and ecclesiastical officials began to lead the masses into the new financial slavery. The first recorded Passion play took place at Siena about 1200,[1] the year when the government of the Italian communes was taken over by the foreign podestas, and about the same time that the old Christian law against usury was disobeyed with the connivance of the Papacy itself.[2]

Of course, Passion plays and masses reach back to very primitive rites—to the wailings of women for the loss of Dionysus,[3] or for the burial of John Barleycorn. These were the forerunners of the Maries mourning at the tomb of Jesus; but the significance of the Passion play from the end of the twelfth century to the time of Bach was much less abstract and ritual in character, much more intense with real feeling and present relation to the common life.

As the attack upon communal Christianity matured in the thirteenth century the rite grew into the more popular form of the Passion play. Then, as those plays were censored and suppressed in succeeding centuries, the realistic play assumed symbolic and indirect forms, being coloured by official influence until what was once performed as a statement of generally acknowledged and contemporary fact—the fact that an honest man will almost assuredly suffer at the hands of dishonest officials—later on applied to a God who had lived in

[1] Chambers, *Medieval Stage*, II, 75.
[2] Thorndike, *Medieval Europe*, pp. 337-9.
[3] Fraser, *The Golden Bough*.

the first three decades of the Christian era, and to a heaven which could only be reached after death.

The latter form of belief of course exists in the Bach passions; but it is modified by the interpolation of solos and chorales which relate the central symbolic tragedy to the lives of the performers themselves, and to the conditions of their own time—so much so that Spitta speaks of these works as a later revival of the medieval mysteries. It is significant that Mendelssohn omitted just these, the more essential numbers, when he revived the St Matthew Passion; and to-day it is these same numbers which are 'cut' to suit the hurry or hypocrisy of Christian audiences.

Within the mysticism and obscurity of Bach's artforms we feel the frustrated passions of the whole people. The later conception of an historical Christ and a spiritual hereafter could not entirely banish the twelfth century belief in the godspring of human beings, and the hope, at least, that earth itself could some day be made a good place for all.

In the Bach Passions the expression is of course conveyed more by means of the music than by the deliberate indirection of the libretto, and by the lyrical solo and choral commentaries which are so much more important and revealing than the actual references to the passion of Christ himself.

Bach gives but a minimum of interest and musical value to the story as such, but he relates it to the life

of his own time by means of the solos, and still more
by means of the chorales which bring even the musically uncultured congregations into the drama. He had
not the physical medium of the stage-play—that had
been forbidden by the Pilates and Caiaphases of the
time as being too politically exciting and dangerous. It
was still used at Oberammergau, and until lately at
Zittau; but generally such an art-form was unrealized
and even useless. Bach needed no physical stage. The
realistic nature of his music brought enough of action
before the imaginative sight of the public, and of inner
mental life it brought much more—an immediate emotional consciousness of the drama as it applied to themselves, the emotions of the drama being made by means
of music actual within the vitals of every performer
and auditor.

Official Protestantism had been faced with the problem of the popular stage much in the same way that
the earlier Catholic Church had been faced with the
problems of pagan ritual. In each case the popular
thing was too strong to be uprooted; so each church
took it over and used it for its own ends, spoiling its
original value by throwing mud upon the manner of
its previous usage. Apollo and Lucifer, gods of light,
were declared, and indeed had become, gods of darkness; so Luther declared that the popular arts should
become 'grave and decent, of course, and not mere

coarse buffoonery, such as they used to be under popery."[1]

The coarse buffoonery which Luther chose to ascribe to the papacy was of course a part of the real and popular nature of the art. The Protestants were not able to get rid of it, and when relics of it appear in Bach's own art we have the merely artistic admirers of his work disapproving of it in the usual official manner —the scribes of a later day repeating the same condemnation of the high priests who had gone before. Bach had to evade the anti-Christian glosses of Lutheranism, as the first Protestants had had to oppose the deceits of decadent Catholicism. It was not that he worked under a kind of ban so far as stage-representation was concerned; he was one of those dramatic artists who had outgrown the need for physical representation just because their sense of drama had become so acute. Much as Gordon Craig stands to the spoken drama of our own day, Bach stood to the Italian opera of his.

The operatic tradition prevailing at Leipsic had almost broken the heart of Kuhnau. The whole of self-respecting Protestantism was up in arms against the tawdriness and insincerity of the opera as they knew it, impoverished as it was by the bored selfishness of the ruling class. But the dramatic spirit is a part of all the most vital art, and lives in some ways even more strongly when the stage is decadent. The dramatic

[1] Michelet's *Luther*, Eng. transl. (Bohn Library), p. 287.

spirit lived in Bach with a greater intensity because he was deprived of the adventitious aids of such a stage. None of the arts using a visible medium were at his disposal; he had therefore to feel with double strength, to develop a kind of aural eye. He had no lighting, and could not bring into visible relief the inscription over the head of the Crucified, but he could imagine an orchestral figure which might serve instead; or a music for darkness, as for example in the middle of the contralto aria, 'It is finished.' He had no stage properties, but he could provide a musical equivalent for the scourging, or a swift-sweeping phrase with one note cut off to make almost visible the sword-stroke of Peter. He had no turbulent stage-crowd; but he could write choruses in which the parts sway in angry agreement, or push and elbow as undirected and excited mobs do everywhere. Like Shakespeare he had no scenery; but just as the poet could afford to despise a moon on a back cloth because he could paint a better moon in words, so Bach could provide a better, and even a moving picture, as in the rending of the veil or the laying of the body in the tomb.

All these, however, are but finer offerings in place of the trappings and trickery of stagecraft. Cleverly as Bach used them, they were but incidental to the motive of his real drama; for, as we have already seen, the representation of the last days of Christ was but a key to the better understanding of the real drama—wherein living Christians suffered the Passion over again.

Consequently in the St John Passion a double drama pursues its way from beginning to end: first a scene from the gospel story, told in simple but veracious recitative; then the more important matter, and application of that scene to the present lives of Christians by means of an aria, or its acceptance by the mass of German believers in terms of folk-song.

The dramatic unity of the work is preserved not only in the natural unfolding of the double drama, but by the repetition and inter-relation of musical numbers, including the congregational chorales.

Such was the work which Bach made during his spare time in the service of a friendly employer. He was not satisfied to sing as a bird in a cage. The whole heart of the man moved out of him towards the greater world of real thought and action, and therefore of more intense art. However comfortable and safe he may have felt in the protection of Prince Leopold, the nature of the artist was such that he *needed* the difficulties and dangers of the larger world where the arts are as real as hunger and war, and not merely pleasant ways of spending empty hours.

ᕽ Chapter Nine ᕽ

BURGHER SERVICE AT LEIPSIG

ACH's biographers seem agreed that the Cöthen period was the happiest of his life. Its termination was due to a variety of reasons. There was a lack of educational facilities for his sons; Prince Leopold took a second wife, and thereafter grew less enthusiastic in matters of music; and after a long spell of sequestered work the master felt the need of public service in which only could his full powers be brought into action.

He would have preferred an appointment which was going at Hamburg; but that was snatched by a musician who was willing to pay for it; so Bach finally decided to take the position of Cantor at St Thomas's, Leipsig. Thus, from being in a protected position where he was able to do almost as he pleased in a little world of pure art, he became a subordinate official and pedagogue in a comparatively large world.

But what a world!

The prince of Anhalt-Cöthen was a superior example of German royalty. As we have seen, the majority of his brother princes were vampires of the worst description.

Lucky the German province where the ruler had a certain degree of good nature.

At this time Saxony was being ruled by Augustus the Strong, regarding whom Carlyle amusingly and contemptuously rhapsodized. That prince had a bevy of mistresses who bled his people white. Instead of patronizing art he patronized artistic debauch. Enormous festivals were organized, and large bodies of soldiers and servants impressed to act dramatic parts upon a Reinhardtian scale. For one firework eighteen thousand trunks of trees were used. For one tapestry six thousand ells of cloth were wasted. Millions of dollars were expended upon a single fete.[1]

Bach's relations with that Gargantuan person were of little account; but, such as they were, they provide some amusement for the student. The composer was not able to get anything out of the prince (who was also King of Poland) in the way of artistic patronage; but he effectually appealed to the royal authority when he found local conditions difficult. He had a taste of the differences existing between the civic and religious authorities at the ceremony of his installation, when the opposed functionaries very nearly came to blows.

From the time of the Reformation there had existed a tug of war between the municipal and ecclesiastical organizations. The Town Councils were keen to maintain all they could of the power the communes had won in

[1] Menzel, III, 18.

the Middle Ages; while the Lutheran officials (from the time they were allied with royalties) took every opportunity of acquiring in Protestant countries the kind of position and influence held in Catholic countries by the Roman clergy.

The dispute at the appointment of Bach seems to have been an example of that opposition, the clerical Consistory demanding a definite part in the ceremony, whereas the townspeople regarded the matter as their own, the presence of the clerics being tolerated merely as an act of courtesy. It is a small matter, but it indicates the undercurrent of antagonism between the two factions which boiled beneath the master's lifework from beginning to end; and by this time he had had about enough of it.

Of course, in such a dispute the royal authority would incline to support the ecclesiastical organization, though it might not be wise to use the partiality too openly. Bach saw his chance, and, when the time came, used the dispute to his own advantage by playing off one set against the other.

At this time Leipsig was an important artistic centre. 'Its public possessed literary interests, and was eager to promote national intellectual culture; and during the first decades of the eighteenth century, Leipsig had reached the standpoint of being the centre of taste which ruled all Germany.'[1] It is the more amazing to

[1] Mantzius, *History of Theatrical Arts*, Eng. transl., V, 33.

learn how backward were the musical conditions which Bach found at the chief church.

His actual position was that of Cantor, teacher of choirboys and director of music, at the church and school of St. Thomas. With that position went certain more or less honorary duties, including those of director of music at the university church of St. Nicholas; and in connection with the university there was a musical society which gave one or two concerts each week.

It seems to have been Bach's policy to develop the honorary parts of the work. In fact he came to look on them as the chief objects of the appointment, and sought to establish in the form of regulary salary such payment as had been made to his predecessor in the form of honorarium. So doing he appealed to the burghers against the clerics, and to the king over the heads of the university authorities; and if he did not gain all he hoped, at any rate he succeeded in improving and enlarging the position for which he was originally engaged.

At the time of his appointment he was generally regarded as one of the chief musicians in northern Germany. He retained the title of honorary Capellmeister to the Prince of Anhalt-Cöthen, and to that was added the title of Capellmeister to the court of Weissenfels, a gay court where the religious part of his nature could certainly find no encouragement. But while he was thus securing himself complaints were made that he neglected the drudgery of the work at St. Thomas's. Because he was Bach we look back with sympathy on his slackness in the training of choirboys. We have the usual regrets that a great artist cannot be placed in a position of pensioned honour, and his work be left to his own will; but we may be wrong. He was originally so anxious to get the appointment that without persuasion he promised to be responsible for the boys' Latin as well as their music and discipline.

Bach lived at that crucial moment in Christian civilization when music was about to leave the sphere of religious expression and pass into the sphere of entertainment. Bach stood to Christian music very much as Aeschylus to Greek drama.[1]

The Cantor had been obliged to sign the Concordia formula, an agreement which betokened the definite subordination of Christian principle to commercial power. Yet he had an inner sense of the great religious work which he was still to do—a work which could not be done in the seclusion of a little court appointment, nor in his new conditions either unless he could manage to shape the material to his need.

The material was unpromising enough. The choirboys were almost beggars, without discipline or musical capacity.

So far we may well sympathize with the creative artist, for he seemed once again faced with a life of

---

[1] See Professor Murray's preface to his translation of the *Agamemnon*.

THE THOMASCHULE IN LEIPSIG, 1723

miserable and almost hopeless drudgery. But the fact remains that he could not have carried out his creative work without that sort of public appointment, however unsatisfactory its details.

None of the greatest artists have continued to create works without relation to the needs of the public. Even Wagner during his exile wrote for the public of a democratic ideal which was not realized in his time. Such necessary relation between great artists and the greater world is not because of anything idle or weak in their own natures. On the contrary, it is because without such a relation their powers cannot be brought into full activity. Great artists are in relation to the greater world of men and women as great ships to the sea; they can only float in deep waters. At all costs the building slips of the shipyard must be related to the movement of the tides, and at all costs the work of great genius must be related to those emotional tides which rise only in a large consensus of human feeling.

Bach's various relations with royal, clerical, and municipal authorities may easily be interpreted to his disadvantage; but his methods of procedure were inevitable if he was to hold that necessary public position and at the same time carry out his equally necessary public function. A refusal to recognize the element of necessity in the production of great art is merely the cynical frame of mind of the man (was it Richelieu?)

who recognized no necessity in the demands of life itself.

That Bach succeeded in his rather devious ways during those early years at Leipsig shows that to the faith of a Christian he was forced to add something of the mentality generally associated with the name of Machiavelli. With the need he had to safeguard his own creative life there was also the need he had to bring up a very large family of children on seven hundred dollars a year.

No wonder that he was forced at times to consider financial matters as of urgent importance, demanding even an appeal for support to a king whom he must have held in contempt and aversion.

For an understanding of his real mind at that time it is necessary, as usual, to study the music which he was producing, and not so much the documents which reveal only the cautious language which he used in his struggles.

The cantata first chosen for his trial service at Leipsig was *Du wahrer Gott und David's Sohn*. It had been composed at Cöthen and represents his innermost feelings during his life there—feelings far removed from the unalloyed happiness which he is supposed to have enjoyed. Its choice was probably due to Bach's feeling as artist, for it is not only suitable in what it reveals of the general Christian faith of that time—

it is also one of the very finest of his earlier cantatas.
For sheer mastery of the webs of polyphony it would
be hard to instance any music more delicately intricate
than the first number, while the references to traditional tunes mark a reversion to the superpersonal feeling which is always to be found in the master's finest
work. But *Du wahrer Gott* is a work of pain, almost of
pessimism; and evidently Bach did not wish to make
that kind of impression at his trial service. Moreover,
the first, and in some ways the most wonderful number, involved the employment of a clever treble soloist,
and he had discovered that his Leipsig boys were
scarcely trustworthy.

So Bach set to work to make a cantata specially for
the occasion; and if the words of *Du wahrer Gott*
accurately express his feelings when deprived of living
Christian intercourse, the words of the cantata *Jesus
nahm zu sich die Zwolfe* no less clearly reveal the
mood in which he took up the new appointment.
Equally with the other cantata is the work one of
pietist tendency. 'Well for me,' says Bach in the second
number, 'if I can thoroughly understand to my comfort
the meaning of this time of suffering and death.' In
the ability of the twelve disciples to understand Christ's
words Bach uses pointed reference to the inability of
the official Lutheran officials to carry out their real
duties. 'There is a longing for the things of the world

and for great houses,'[1] says Bach, for the libretto is almost certainly his own. But he will not end on a note of disheartenment, and in the final chorale we get an echo of medieval hope, expressing the will that 'the new life may come even here on this earth.'

This cantata is apparently harder, but actually easier to perform than the work first chosen. The difficulties are almost entirely in the organ part, and that Bach evidently filled out himself at the time, much of it having been left by him in a skeleton form. Then it needs a smaller orchestral body, and has no treble solo part for incompetent boyhood to spoil. From the vocal point of view *Jesus nahm* is more grateful to sing in the chorus as well as the solo parts; and though it touches moods of deepest pathos it ends with the sort of chorus which sends away an audience in good spirits.

Carlyle said that the chief function of music is to utter the praise of God. Hugo Wolf gave expression to the same idea when he said that music reaches its highest powers in exultation. We have already learned that Bach knew the depths of sorrow, and was very ready to express them; but, given a real chance, no composer soars to such heights of joy as he, and in some of the early Leipsig compositions he makes trial flights. The most definite of these is his setting of the *Magnifi-*

[1] The building of big houses for rich burghers was as typical of the so-called Renaissance as the building of cathedrals in the 12th and 13th centuries.

cat. In that work and in certain numbers from the cantatas *Die Elenden sollen essen* and *Die Himmel erzahlen* there is rapturous music; and if the early works of the Cöthen years expressed the happy relief he then felt in his first taste of congenial material conditions, in these early Leipsig works there is the nobler relief of an artist who has now the chance to express ideas which have too long been denied utterance.

The first cantata actually composed at Leipsig has reference to the subject of Dives and Lazarus, a subject so dear to the hearts of the people everywhere that they have themselves made folk-songs upon it. In such ways was Bach forced from within to identify himself with the common people of Christendom and of Leipsig. And in that, as in most of the early Leipsig cantatas, the importance of the chorale, the people's own song, is reasserted. Certain recitatives are included (inserted by Bach himself?) with a very plain meaning. Unfortunately for English people most of those recitatives are translated with so obviously weakened a meaning that their original intention has scarcely been appreciated. Thus Bach's *Was hilft des Purpurs Majestät*, which I suppose is the German equivalent for 'What avails the royal purple' is given in one English translation as 'What profiteth pomp's high estate?' Thus is Bach's deliberate meaning glossed. Such phrases are important as indicating Bach's opinions. The one just quoted does not stand alone. In *Die Himmel erzahlen*

Professor Terry with a fairer courage translates as follows:

> Our men of wit do folly talk
> And Belial's form in God's own house doth stalk;

and many thoughts akin to those are evidence of the pietist or popular core of Bach's art, however he may have been forced for the sake of his livelihood to pretend a more orthodox belief.

Bach produced those first two Leipsig cantatas, and then there was a sudden change of librettist. Perhaps someone in authority was not entirely pleased with the thoughts expressed by the new Cantor.

The cantatas which followed were apparently not to words selected by the composer himself, but the 'unknown librettist' continued to insert surprising recitatives—a little more cautiously perhaps, not in such a way as might upset officially sensitive persons, but definitely stating ideas like those we have learned to associate with Bach himself. Thus in the cantata which immediately followed the two above-mentioned the Cantor seemed to be directing his thoughts at the very people who had objected to the real Christianity of his previous works. 'Hypocrisy is a foul spawn. . . . Can it be that Christians are to that evil tempted? . . . Yes, some with natures devilish outward as angels seem. . . . Calumny, hate, back-biting, abuse and jealous slighting are their besetting sin.'[1]

[1] Terry, *Bach Cantata Texts*, p. 341.

One or two further outbursts Bach permitted himself in the cantatas generally credited to his first year at Leipsig, notably in the Good Samaritan cantata (No. 164) in which he turns and fairly lashes his opponents; but for the rest he settles down into a heaven-in-the-sweet-bye-and-bye frame of mind, and gives his inmost feelings rather in the music than the words. Thus there is the angry music to the words 'Fret not thyself, O soul,' in Cantata 186. When a man utters such words in accents of fury we have either to look upon the matter as a joke, or understand that the occasion is serious and indignation cannot or will not be easily suppressed. This number exactly gives Bach's own frame of mind. He was realizing bitterly but very definitely that for him to insist on giving out in clear and open terms the truth that was in him would mean his own complete suppression. Things had come to such a pass that a Christian might no longer advocate Christianity except in the way of hypocrisy. In his Good Samaritan cantata he had cried out, 'Ye who call upon Christ's name, where is your love and charity'; and again 'Only by love and charity are we made Godlike,' which seems another way of expressing Blake's idea of the nature of divinity:—'Jesus is the only god, and so am I, and so are you.' That seems to have been Bach's last verbal statement of his belief, for that year at any rate. As Blake concealed his ideas in an obscure and monstrous mythology, Bach concealed his more effectively and more beautifully in music. Whenever thereafter he was able to emphasize his belief indirectly he did so. For example, when he wrote a cantata for the newly elected Town Council, he (again like Blake) referred to his city as Jerusalem; but as the poet associated the city with England's green and pleasant land, so Bach associated his Jerusalem with such lines as 'O dwellers by the lime trees,' the lime trees of Leipsig, and showed once again that for him religion was not a matter of the skies only, not a matter of the past history of Syria, nor a matter of the hereafter when he would be gone; but a very present concern of the life he was sharing with his fellow citizens.

Nevertheless, from that time onwards, for the expression of the real Bach and his time, we must look chiefly to his music, and above all to the increasing importance which he gives to the chorales. By his use of the people's own songs and dance-rhythms he continued to maintain contact with the spirit of his religion as it had flowered most wonderfully in the Middle Ages. From that time until his death the chorale is the kernel of his work, and its influence is to be found even in the so unlikely a place as his setting of the Latin *Magnificat*.

The form in which we now have Bach's *Magnificat* does not give his real and original idea of the work. For him it was almost dramatic in form, its performance at Christmas being traditionally associated in the church with the actual rocking of the baby Christ's cradle, German interpolations being added to the Latin text the more definitely to point the real and present meaning of the work. In that way it corresponds to the bilingual carols which Protestant peoples maintained against official attempts to insist on the foreign and generally meaningless tongue. Even as we have Bach's *Magnificat*, there remains the beautiful *Suscepit* with its chorale *in the instrumental part*, and the gusto with which the music lays tremendous emphasis on the antithesis of rich and poor, mighty and meek. Once again it must be noted that the effect is obtained less by the words than by the emotion of the music itself.

One other lovely and significant work belongs to 1723, the motet, *Jesu meine Freunde*. It was written for the funeral of the wife of one of the master's old friends at Cöthen.

Bach had now reached the fullness of his power, and had taken fair measures of what he could and could not do in the irreligious circumstances of his time. He was thirty-eight years of age, and had written about a third of his complete output. The remaining two-thirds were to be composed during the next twenty-seven years of his life.

The long and amazing period of productivity which followed cannot be traced here in any detail, nor is such a course necessary for this particular study. It remains therefore to record the few, mostly unpleasant, incidents of his life at Leipsig, and to indicate the outstanding features of his mature work. The great bulk of his church cantatas was still to come, and they have yet to be examined in relation to his detailed development. That would take us far beyond the limits of a book of this kind. Those cantatas, with the two Passions and the B minor Mass, definitely establish the fundamental Christianity and dramatic genius of the master according to the principles already outlined.

The order in which the cantatas were written has been suggested by Spitta, and confirmed or corrected by Schweitzer, Prout, and Terry. Their reckoning gives thirty-seven cantatas to the years 1724-1727, and one hundred and twenty-two (including the Christmas Oratorio) to the last part of Bach's life. The two groups are divided by the composition of the St Matthew Passion, while the later cantatas mostly cover the period in which the B minor Mass was undergoing its process of slow accretion.

As an example of Bach's will to relate his superb technical mastery to his conception of service in the popular cause, while making allowance for the peculiar difficulties against which he had to strive during his earlier years at Leipsig, let us examine the cantata *Christ lag in Todesbanden*. It belongs to the second year of his cantorship when he had ceased to struggle outwardly against the deadening influence of orthodoxy.

The words were Luther's own, so no one would object to them. The inefficiency of the choirboys had to be considered, so the difficulty of the treble line was reduced to a minimum. Of the seven sections only one has a treble line of any difficulty so far as the chorus is concerned, and only one other any difficulty for a solo treble, while the worst difficulties were lightened by the fact that the entire work is really a series of variations upon the original hymn-tune, a tune which everybody knew already, and would with the greater interest follow in the masterly musical changes presented by Bach—the imitative passages in diminution succeeded by an amazing ragtime Hallelujah chorus, the powerful bass figure for man's bondage to death in pre-Christian times, the laughing joyousness which accompanies the breaking of the bonds, the almost physical struggle between life and death, and when it would seem that nothing of happiness remained to be expressed the new waves of joy which arrive in a change of superficial rhythm.

This work is particularly notable because of a splendid example of the cumulative climax in the first chorus. To-day that sort of climax is expected as a matter of course; it is the most exciting sort of effect in choral and orchestral writing, and once the trick is learned is fairly easy to manage. Because Bach used it on this occasion so magnificently it may be worth while asking why he did not use that kind of effect more often.

All the greatest art in the world will, I think, be found to have a static quality so powerful that its climactic point is unobserved, because definitely subordinate to the complete conception. Unless for technical reasons we deliberately seek it out we are not specially aware of the highest light in a great picture, or the climax of a fine piece of music; we accept the climax in relation to the work as a whole. If we do become aware of a climax as such it means that our attention has been drawn from the central significance of the art-work. Third-rate artists make us aware of their climax by saving it up for the very end of a poem or piece of music, or by stabbing our sight with a high light out of graduated relation to the rest of the picture. First-rate artists almost always coax our sight by degrees, or in music and literature allow themselves room to relieve the passion which may be aroused by the climax. Bach's carelessness, not to say contempt, for effects of climax, was such that in his cantatas the most powerful moment nearly always comes in the first number, generally a chorus which states the central idea of the whole cantata; what follows is the detail which flows from that greatest moment. It is the feature of his work which, more than any other, causes us to feel its sculptural quality.

Musical art which has become only a form of idle amusement has always a great need for climaxes— more and more of them, till we scarcely know where

we are, but are carried away with the nervous excite-
ment of it all. It is therefore rather the characteristic
of a decadent age when a feeling for what is beautiful
needs at best the sort of whip which a climax applies,
and at worst the æsthetic analogy of noisy intoxication.
Finally it defeats its own end, and we have the sort
of 'art' which in our time is not even content to be called
Modern, but demands to be called Futurist as it staggers
down into the pit—drunk in the early morning, nosing
for climax before work has even begun.

The number of duets for treble and alto which Bach
wrote about this time seems to show that he was really
taking pains to improve his boys' singing. His solos
were nearly always for alto, tenor, or bass during the
early Leipsig years; but if he could not trust any of his
boys with a solo he at least began to use one or more
of them in the stricter harness of concerted numbers.
Moreover, duets for treble and alto would enable him
to teach them all something during those practices
which were unattended by adult members of the choir.
Some of the cantatas certainly contain treble lines, and
especially treble chorus lines, of considerable difficulty;
but on the whole he stuck to the plan of giving to
the top line of his great choruses the simple statement
of a chorale which would already be known; and the
plan influenced him to the end of his days. For us it
has the defect that it does not fairly employ the
sopranos of our modern choral societies. For Bach it had

the advantage that he had the less need to give time to the drudgery of practice. He could in his own compositions cover up the deficiencies of his boy singers by the general splendour of his choral and organ technic; but that was a method which did not give any opportunity for improvement in what was the essential weakness of his own choir, and the Town Council soon began to raise objections.

The Council complained that the Cantor was neglecting his duties. Bach replied to the effect that when boys were chosen for admittance to the School of St. Thomas no sufficient consideration was given to their musical capabilities.

Besides the limitations which the master suffered in that regard there were serious orchestral deficiencies.

Among his duties was that of giving instruction to such boys as seemed likely to shape as instrumentalists; and that was a very meagre field for hopeful work. Indeed from the composer's own point of view the situation must have seemed preposterous, the more so because he was even then engaged upon the St Matthew Passion. To make matters worse Bach had quarrelled with some of his colleagues, musical and clerical. He had been unjustly treated quite early on being superseded in a minor duty by a very minor musician. As it had involved the loss of actual money Bach had appealed to the king, and the authorities had been forced to compromise. Then the Cantor got into the sort of dispute between parson and organist which goes on to this day, regarding the choice of music. It would almost seem that the diplomatic qualities the composer had shown in his efforts to get his own way did not extend to the constant suavity of manner required to keep himself in good report. That, I think, in the obverse and unhappy side of a genius which needed for its fair development both public position and private retirement. During the composition of such a work as the St Matthew Passion everything in the nature of public duty must have seemed a dead-weight, everything in the nature of musical drudgery a positive torture.

We may well ask ourselves why, having written so beautiful a work as the St John Passion, Bach should think it necessary to make another music of the same kind. Part of the need may have arisen in the fact that he was expected to provide a continuous succession of compositions for each church year.

Neither Bach himself nor his contemporaries had the pretentious idea that art-works are immortal. Art was still a healthy activity by means of which the human organism threw off leaves and flowers and seeds of the mind, and for each successive season there was naturally a new flowering. With our later and degenerate conception of the nature of inspiration an ordered output of art-works may seem cold-blooded and opposed to the nature of artistic genius. We have the amazing mass of Bach's warm-blooded music to prove the contrary. Handel also was wonderfully fertile, but a very much smaller proportion of his work carries the proof of its inspired quality.

What then do we mean by inspiration?

The romantic idea is that a certain type of mentality, called the creative or artistic genius, is suddenly possessed by a good or evil spirit, whereupon the mortal artist becomes a sort of spiritualistic medium and capable of translating into material forms ideas or suggestions which have their origin in another world than this.

The impersonal element which undoubtedly exists in the work of the greatest artists does not however derive from another world: it arises in the fact that emotions which are experienced by a great number of people at the same time are extraordinarily increased in pressure in the separate persons who make up that number, and especially in those who work in emotional materials. The heightened moods of an excited crowd are, I suggest, only a more vulgar example of the fevers which, transmuted into ordered sound and colour, result in works of inspiration.

Under such pressure the impossible becomes possible, as when the Bastille was stormed and taken by the French people. Carlyle's comment regarding that occasion is very much to the point: 'Hast thou considered how each man's heart is so tremulously responsive

to the hearts of all men? How their shriek of indignation palsies the strong soul; their howl of contumely
withers with unfelt pangs? The Ritter Gluck confessed
that the ground-tone in the noblest passage of one of
his noblest operas was the voice of the populace he
heard at Vienna crying to their Kaiser, Bread, bread!
Great is the combined voice of men; the utterance
of their instincts which are truer than their thoughts;
it is the greatest a man encounters among the sounds
and shadows which make up this world of time.'

A gathered fury may find a massed physical expression as in the taking of the Bastille, and no single person
stand as hero of the occasion; but a gathered emotion
baulked of its natural crisis may miss physical expression
and yet, in the mind of a sympathetic person reach a
certain outlet. Then it may appear as if the expression
is due almost entirely to the 'greatness' of the person
who expressed it, whereas, as in Bach's case, it is but
the conductor which takes the lightning charge. The
emotions of the revolt against the betrayal of Christianity were proved first and physically in the Peasants
War and the contemporary revolts throughout Christendom. Deeds of mass-heroism were then done comparable to the taking of the Bastille. When the crisis
had passed, and the physical revolt had been suppressed,
the emotions still lingered; but having no hopeful
means of expression in action, those emotions were conducted into such channels as popular songs, hymns,

and works of fine art. It is those emotions of the suppressed reality of Christianity which have remained as the motive force of the greatest European art to this day.

So long as there was any present reality or possibility of the general acceptance of Christian principles as the basis of civilization, so long did the worship of the Holy Family at the Christmas celebration remain the centre of popular expression in art, and therefore of what we call inspiration. But when Christendom had been conquered in the association of human greed with the genius for government, the chief celebration of the popular Christian year was transferred from Christmas to Black Friday when the noblest conceivable human being suffered for taking the popular side against the powers of established religion and government.

Venice, the last of the medieval communes to endure, produced so late as 1500 the pictures of Giovanni Bellini in one of which the chief of the government kneels in a worship to a peasant girl and her baby. That was the expression of the mass-feeling in Venice even in the fifteenth century. But in Bach's day the prevailing mass-expression was one of defeat; and so whereas for Christmas he wrote only a number of occasional church cantatas (and those partly adaptations from earlier and even secular works), for the celebration of what remained real in Christianity he wrote Passions—not one, but four.

Of the four two survive. They belong to periods
when the master himself was in an abnormal state of
emotional life. At Cöthen, where he had no outlet for
his most intense feelings but the vague suggestiveness
of instrumental forms, he produced the vivid Passion
according to St. John. At Leipsig during the years
of his struggle with the Town Council for the dignity
and financial rights of his office, he composed the calmer
and more deeply rooting work according to St. Matthew.

Schweitzer says that the Jesus of the St. Matthew
Passion is more human than the Jesus of the St. John.
If so it is not due to any of the words or musical
phrases allotted to the central character, but to the
string accompaniment with which the part is associated
in the later work, and even more to the fact that in the
St. Matthew the significance of the character is trans-
mitted, even more than in the St. John by the actual
singers and especially (note the fact) by the chorus.

In the greater Passion the soloists are more closely
bound up with the choristers. There are no fewer than
six very important numbers for soloist *and* chorus—a
fact which may cause us to recall the relation between
solo and tutti in the concertos. Then several of the arias
are marked to be sung by Chorus I or Chorus II,
though I am not sure whether that was meant to indicate that a whole section of the chorus should sing
the aria, or merely that the soloist should be drawn

from this or that side of the church choir. In any case it is clear that the essential drama of the work, which in the St. John Passion we found to exist chiefly in the arias, has in the St. Matthew Passion been subtly transferred to the choral mass. This seems to have been no mere predilection for choral tone, but an artistic expression of the great religious fact of Bach's time, the Passion of the people themselves. The choruses which are set to gospel words are short and almost incidental in the St. Matthew Passion. If stage performances were in question they would be more manageable in the St. Matthew than in the St. John choruses; nevertheless the stage drama is even more removed from the later than from the earlier work. The St. John Passion approached the whole story much more objectively, and, except for the arias, more historically. The later Passion is more subjective throughout, and refers to the historical Jesus only with sufficient emphasis to relate the symbol to the religious reality in Bach's own time. In the earlier work the central figure is set up as a special example to Christians of all time, and dominates the whole drama; in the later work the central interest passes from the personality of Jesus to those actually engaged in the act of musical worship.

For us that may be a little hard to appreciate because both Passions have become works of art first of all, and remain works of religion only in an historical sense; while as for having any real validity as the expression of our own beliefs and actions—that is ruled out of account by the whole tendency of modern life in all so-called Christian countries. We hear those Passions in concert-rooms, and call the occasions 'performances.' More rarely they are given in churches, but only as special events, not because they serve the urgent need of any of the ecclesiasticized bodies— Roman, Anglican, Nonconformist, Jewish, Christian Scientist, or any other.

A more real—or if you will, a more musical—Christianity existed in Bach's day, troubled and suppressed though it was. Works like the Passions were a vital part of the life of the cultured community; and it would seem that there was a greater number of ordinary men and women capable of appreciating such works. The growth of mechanized industry has been associated with a growth of population, but there is now a smaller proportion of folk who can without special technical study appreciate these religious works of Bach, and a still smaller proportion of singing folk who can perform them with the amount of preliminary study given by the forces at the disposal of the master of Leipsig. It shows a real lack of understanding of the nature of the works when, as at our chief musical festivals, they are included in programmes cheek by jowl with the ironies of modern music. In Bach's day the only place for the Mass was the Mass-service, and the only place for the Passions was the great annual act of worship which had its roots in the most primitive rite of spring, and was regularly celebrated on the day called Good Friday.

Therefore to appreciate this Passion as it sprang from the mind of its composer it is necessary that we forget every concert-performance we have ever heard, and try to approach it as the Leipsig congregation approached it when they assembled to do their part—humble, but none the less musical and real—in the church of St. Thomas in 1729.

The opening chorus gives the clue to the work. One group of singers is invited by another group to share their sorrow, insisting upon its present nature, not referring to Christ as a personage who had lived in the past, but as to one who is living with them in the present. They emphasize the actuality of the occasion by appealing, not to history or memory, but to sight. 'See Him,' 'Look, for love of us His cross He is bearing!' This is not a Christ who died in Jerusalem centuries ago, but a Christ who was bearing his cross then and there with the Leipsigers themselves. Those who sang were men and women of Saxony, calling to each other as they gathered together from the two sides of the street.

After the extraordinary reality of that opening chorus the gospel narrative in recitative seems curiously remote and unreal. That unreality is emphasized by the chorale which follows; and whether or not the chorale was sung (as I believe) by the congregation itself, the mere usage of the popular tune was enough to draw their feelings into the work in a more intimate way. The greater musical beauty of the chorus and chorale on either side of the incidental recitative is of itself enough to show where the real meaning of the work lies. If to that you answer that it proves the work to be one merely of musical art and not of religion it will be honest of you, but scarcely satisfactory in a civilization which still calls itself Christian.

That the chorales were meant to be sung by the congregation at large has been disputed. But imagine at the present day a large body of people hearing a tune well known to them. If there is nothing to prevent them, a few will begin to hum the tune, then more and more, until sooner or later they break into the actual words.

Had Bach intended to have checked that tendency we may be sure that he would have used tunes less generally known; but that would have made an end of the Passion service as he conceived it, which apparently was to keep aglow in the minds of his fellows the idea that in every person there existed the possibility of moral growth and physical courage like that symbolized by the story of Christ—a morale which in earlier centuries had saved Western Europe from imperial decadence and feudal anarchy. Whether it would save them from the new anarchy that was coming upon them in the guise of a mechanical civilization, or from the new financial despotism, was another matter. Of those evils the masses of men were suspicious, though not fully aware; and they were certainly incompetent then to save themselves. But it was to preserve their essential Christian brotherhood in face of an evil which they had begun to fear, but did not fully understand, that many of them had got into the habit of meeting together in religious services such as these Passions.

The same choristers who at one moment were singing words of Christian devotion were presently singing the anti-Christianity of priests, especially 'chief priests' (I suppose to-day they would be called bishops), 'scribes' (leader-writers?) and elders of the people (aldermen and councillors?) The double role was no mere economy of musical forces. Bach had already divided his choralists into two; had he chosen he could have named one group for the sinners and the other for the saints. But was it not an essential principle of Christianity that the opposing powers of good and evil were present in every single human being, awaiting only conditions of advantage for development? Was not the Christian fight taking place, not only between those who were acting for or against Christian principle, but also to a lesser extent in the hearts of each separate Christian?

Is such a Passion-drama less dramatic because its life

is internal, its action unstageable, and its characters all Everymans?

Every time the singers declared the Pharisaical virtues of those who rebuked an act of love in the name of prudence or alms-giving, they were declaring vices which rose in their own hearts.

Every time they sang of the treachery of Judas it was of a treachery which was always possible because of the weakness of themselves. Notice that the sorrowful chorus, 'Is it I?' of the historical disciples is followed by the more real chorus of the Leipsicers—'*My* sin it is which binds thee.'

However, it was not only the vices of the anti-Christian spirit which they realized as rampant in their recent and contemporary history; it was also the possibilities they carried within themselves of struggling for a Christian world. Thus, the Agony in the Garden having been introduced by formal reminder of gospel narrative, there follows the wonderful piece for tenor solo and chorus which transmutes it from an historical or legendary thing to an individual and general experience.

Continually in the course of the work it happens that the idea raised by the story, and made vital and moving by the quality of the music, becomes essentially a topical affair.

Christ bound and led in procession through the city has choral cries of 'Loose him! Leave him! Bind Him not!' Rather a different procession to the one which happened a few years earlier at Thorn! For, in the words of Blake, 'this history has been adopted by both parties.' At Thorn the procession celebrated the importance of the symbol in the degradation, increased suffering, and martyrdom of living human beings. In the work of Bach the procession celebrated the importance of the human beings in the light of all that the symbol implied of gentleness and endurance.

Again, the aria which follows the remorse of Judas, and introduces a wild and passionate sense of loss is no mere condemnation of an historical and single act of betrayal. That would have represented the usual shifting of responsibility from real to symbolic shoulders; and though that plan is entirely true to what remains of modern orthodoxy, it was quite contrary to the spirit of the noblest religious art from the twelfth century to the time of Bach.

Yet again, the scourging which in the St. John Passion was a realistic portrayal of physical action, becomes in the St. Matthew Passion the scourging of the worshipping Christians themselves. In the tenor aria, No. 41, it had been significantly and almost secretly transferred by the actual musical phraseology. Later in the work Bach followed his usual plan: first a bare narrative statement of the symbolic occurrence, then its more rhythmic statement in topical form, and then in most beautiful musical form its real application to life, with the suggestion that pity for the scourged Christ is not required of the Leipsigers, but rather their maintenance of Christian principle in face of ridicule—that more modern form of scourging in an anti-Christian world.

Bach's genius reached its culmination in the St. Matthew Passion. He was yet to complete a more imposing music, but the great Passion is the work in which the living spirit of Christianity is most definitely related to the actual life of his time. As a work of art it is as nearly perfect as we are likely to know. There is no pause in its steady dramatic development, while the passage from symbolic creed to real and urgent principle is maintained without effort or emphasis.

In one of his many flashes of clarity Blake sang:

> I will not cease from mental fight,
> Nor shall my sword sleep in my hand,
> Till I have built Jerusalem
> In England's green and pleasant land.

Bach sang the same battle song for the Leipsigers. He declared the complete field and detail of their battle-drama in one continuous searchlight of song. And there are no places where the light is thrown unnecessarily: contrarily to a common belief, this is not a work which can be intelligently given in mutilated form. There are a few phrases where a strict adherence to words of the Bible introduces unnecessary allusions, but they are only slight and passing. The essence of the work lies in the arioso numbers, the arias, and the choruses, and of these—contrary to what even so great an authority as Elgar has proposed—not one can be omitted without injuring the original and essential purpose of the work.[1] It is better to perform this Passion in its separate parts entire, or even in its separate scenes, than to promise the whole work and then, by omitting certain numbers, make it endurable for minds which may be offended by its length or its Christianity.

Bach can have had few illusions regarding the kind of performance which awaited the work. Vivid as were the conceptions within his own mind, the human material of his choir and his instrumental forces were unequal to the occasion. Of the latter he said 'diffidence forbids my speaking truly of their quality and musical knowledge.' His regular orchestra consisted of two violins, two oboes, two trumpets, and a bassoon; and there exists a report which he submitted to the Town Council stating that the least of his additional needs were a double quartet of strings, a double bass, two flutes, drums, a third oboe or taille (English horn) and a third trumpet. Lacking these instruments the composer had to get what he could of additional help from his boys; and if he had proved unequal to their

[1] The edition of Sir Edward Elgar and Sir Ivor Atkins is the best available for use in an English translation, and is of service in making the various sections clear. Its errors seem to me to lie in the proposal above indicated, and in the use of a hymn (No. 63) from the Roman liturgy—that is actually opposed to the spirit of Bach's conception.

control and training in the matter of singing, we can imagine that the result was even less satisfactory in the more difficult business of instrumental tuition.

In the year of the production of the St. Matthew Passion he was appointed conductor of the Telemann Singing Society, a university organization devoted chiefly to the performance of instrumental and secular music; and he may have had its help in the Passion service. That would explain some things in the orchestration of his chief work, including the double string orchestra. But whether he had such help or not the general impression made by this greatest of all religious choral works seems to have been somewhat negative; and the gloom which settled upon Bach after that time is something of an indication that the greatest achievement of his life had been little appreciated.

Nor can we be surprised at that, for the Passion had emphasized every aspect of Christianity which the respectable bourgeois Council were intent on ignoring, and if possible reinterpreting in their own middle-class interest.

The next year brought matters to a head.

Chapter Ten

THE LAST LONELINESS

IN THE cantata, *Ein feste Burg*, Bach foreshad-
owed the great series of chorale-cantatas
which more than any other works after the
St. Matthew Passion prove his inmost fidelity to his
original principles. *Ein feste Burg* was written to cele-
brate the bicentenary of the Reformation itself, and is
built upon one of the most popular Lutheran hymns.
For it Bach used words which attacked the ideas of the
official class, declaring that it was his job 'to serve
Christ and not another.' His enemies chose, not the un-
orthodox spirit of the work, but its inevitably poor
performance, as their line for an attack upon him.
Bach's reply was to put in the report from which a
quotation has been made in the previous chapter. That
report used none of the servile terminology to which
the burghers, now *nouveaux riches*, were becoming accustomed. Their answer was of the sort which they
have used down to our own day: they found a way of
clipping his livelihood.

Certain extra moneys had in the past been divided
between the various officials of St. Thomas's School.

JOHN SEBASTIAN BACH
Sculpture by Georg Kolbe

That year when the others had their shares Bach was ignored. He was left with his bare salary, while a growing family was demanding ever more of life's material things.

At first it was as if his creative genius had received a blow: what had hitherto been a torrent of religious and musical productivity suddenly dwindled into a thin trickle of minor pieces, the compulsory cantatas often being arranged from previously written secular and instrumental music. Schweitzer shows unnecessary astonishment at the quality of these works, and calls them 'disappointing.'[1] The heart had temporarily ceased to function in the master's work, and he sometimes provided only the merest thread of musical texture.

Three years were largely occupied in an attempt to get an appointment elsewhere. In Leipsig itself much of his energy was given to the Telemann Society. For that he made secular cantatas and concertos, including rearrangements of some of his Cöthen music.

Most interesting of those pieces from a biographical point of view is Phoebus and Pan. It proved the combative vitality of the master. In the moment of his deep anxiety and depression he was able with no small fund of musical wit to enter the lists against a critic who was using the period of Bach's unpopularity with the officials to wound him still further. The question involved was the relative values of simple folk-spirit in

[1] Schweitzer, II., 237-9.

music and a more fully developed intellectual and emotional art. Bach is absolutely fair in his presentation of the controversy; and to this day when we hear the music it is hard to agree with the verdict. While appreciating all that Bach offers in the songs of Phoebus and Tmolus in the way of Apollonian beauty, many will feel with Nietzsche that there is even more to be said for the Dionysian songs of Pan and poor old long-eared Midas—and the composer's judgment seems the harder to support because to the Dionysian songs Bach added all he knew of suitable art derived from the Apollonian source itself!

This burst of hearty laughter in the midst of grave trouble is some measure of the moral strength of the master; and fortunately help was approaching from an unexpected quarter.

A new rector was appointed—one Gesner, who had known Bach at Weimar, and had there learned to excuse the petty angularities and deficiencies of the musician's character for the sake of the sincerity and genius.

Gesner quickly made it his business to intervene on Bach's behalf with the Council, and the extra monies were once more forthcoming. It was lucky, for the efforts Bach had made to get an appointment elsewhere had met with little success, and he was already feeling his way towards a very different kind of support in his struggle with the burghers. If he could not secure the welfare of his family in the straight way of his work he must seek it at the hands of some authority which the burghers dare not question.

When Augustus, the much bemistressed Saxon king, succeeded in mounting the Polish throne, he had had to foreswear his Protestant pretendings. That had been resented by his Saxon subjects, and his queen chose that particular moment to dissociate herself from him. She was accordingly accounted a heroine and almost a martyr by the people, and when she died in 1727 their feelings for her were expressed in a very definite manner. Bach stood in with the people, that time without any need for symbolization or subterfuge, and commemorated her death in a most beautiful Funeral Music —a work which later on significantly became the basis of one of the lost Passions.[1]

The apostate king died in 1733. His successor, also an Augustus, was a young man from whom better things were hoped; still, as Polish king he was necessarily a member of the Roman Church, and it was to gain *his* support against a possible recurrence of civic animosity that Bach began the composition of his B minor Mass.

A superficial knowledge of the history of that time might leave us with the impression that the Mass represented a broadening of Bach's own faith. The whole

[1] Whether the 'loss' of that Passion was an accident, or due to one who would save the master's memory in the eyes of predominant orthodoxy, or even destroy the work as too powerful an expression of popular Christianity, it is impossible to say.

nature of his work shows that he realized how, in the matter of the public welfare, there was little to choose between Roman Peter and Protestant Paul. When any question of action or reality was involved both theologies were on the side of the dominant class and against the people. So Bach might have thought—as many good men have thought since his time—that truth and goodness must be sought backwards in point of time, back to the centuries before Christendom had been divided.

A little more knowledge of the facts will of course inform us that the division of Christianity was not into two but into three, for there was also the Greek Church to tell of a yet earlier division.

A little more history again, and we shall be shown how every church has been organized for the people and largely by their own agency; though sooner or later their clerical officials have been suborned to betray the organization into the hands of the ruling class.

Such historical knowledge may not have been available for Bach; but an instinctive idea of the nature of the betrayal was common throughout Christendom, and, as we have already seen, formed the essential vitality of the Pietist movement, thus also forming the essential vitality of Bach's own art. But that vitality entered into the B minor Mass only indirectly; for the immediate purpose of the work was neither the service of the people nor of their god. Its primary intention was to prove to the Elector of Saxony and King of Poland that its composer was a musical artist of first-rate skill, fit to be engaged for the most important service.

At first glance it may seem strange that the composer of the St. Matthew Passion and the Chorale-Cantatas, with all that they implied of popular feeling, should react to the very extreme of ecclesiastical and royal service. Bach was in a very hard position. He was good for nothing but music. He was prevented from using his only power. It was not only a question of life and death for his art as he conceived it, but of actual livelihood for himself and family. If he submitted to the mean and treacherous will of the burghers he would so lose caste in his own heart that his creative spirit would be quenched. If he did not submit he would be deprived of the means of earning a fair living. In such circumstances he preferred to serve one whose ideals were openly opposed to his own, rather than the dull and irreligious traitors who were building up a new hell upon earth in the name of Protestantism. Could he but gain the goodwill of the open enemy by an act of occasional service, he could quietly continue his own work along the only lines which afforded him power and inspiration; for however much he might be bullied by the burghers so long as he propagated popular doctrines in his works, they would not dare to damage him if he were supported by a still higher authority.

For the precious Protestant officials were themselves generally glad to come to terms with sovereign powers.

In 1733 the first two sections of the Mass were written, and application made by the composer for 'a patent as Predicate of the Court Chapel' in return for what he himself described as 'the accompanying trifling work.' The appointment was not actually made until 1736, and in the meantime the new Rector had sufficiently eased the situation at Leipsig for Bach to resume the normal outflow of composition. That outflow branched out into two definite directions: on the one hand a series of cantatas largely for solo voice wherein the Cantor was able to ignore the deficiencies of the local material, and on the other hand a resumption of chorale-preludes for organ and the beginning of a series of chorale-cantatas of which *Ein Feste Burg* was the forerunner. In these latter works Bach poured out all that was best and noblest during his last years.

Other music was written—secular cantatas, the second part of the Forty-eight, and concerted works, probably for the Telemann Society—but the real nature of Bach was expressed for the rest of his days in the works of which the people's songs are the musical mainstay and the people's longings the inner motive.

Personal troubles were by no means over. Gesner was soon succeeded by a less pleasant Rector who lost no opportunity of making petty difficulties for his Cantor, humiliations which were the easier to effect because of Bach's own hasty temper. But to set against that he had the background of royal support, and that made his enemies more wary in their dealings; and in his own home, and especially in his second wife, he had a real musical as well as domestic anchorage. What he owed to Anna Magdalena we can only guess by the number of his works which exist in her handwriting, and by our knowledge that many pieces were composed for her, sung and played by her. So with a fair idea of the master's physical and mental surroundings, all we have to do is to glance at the chief fruit of his genius during his last years.

Shorn of the urgent emotional impulse which produced the St. Matthew Passion and other works of a similar tendency, Bach naturally concentrated on his craftsmanship in the B minor Mass and other pieces presently to be mentioned. No music can be entirely emotionless and live, and Bach had such a religious and sincere background to his life that even in a work composed to attract notice from King Augustus there are deep emotional values; but the beauty of the Mass lies chiefly in its architectonic proportions, and in the consummate skill with which Bach marshalls every musical detail at his disposal.

I have said that for Bach Passions and Masses were religious services rather than works of art. That is to some extent even true of the *Mass* in *B minor*; but it is not fitted for the ceremonial of the Catholic Sacrament, and certainly not for the service as modified by the Lutherans. For the first it is too deep, for the other too broad. The Mass service for which this work was written was entirely personal to Bach; in it he is chiefly concerned in developing his mastery to its highest technical point. Whatever of vital force the Mass possesses derives from a depth beyond personal understanding; and that derivation is such as causes Bach to give to his *Gloria* the rhythm of a country dance, to his *Et Resurrexit* the measure of a Polonaise,[1] and to his *Et in spiritum sanctum* the mood of a folk-song.

The dramatic nature of the Mass is obvious: its deeper roots are less obvious.

We are told that one of the motives of cannibalism is the intention of acquiring the vital characteristics of the eaten enemy. Among more civilized peoples a finer feeling of worship has entered into the eating of bread which so obviously changes into human flesh, the flesh of the eater, and the drinking of wine which so obviously increases the blood pressure of the drinker. John Barleycorn was the English folk-god of the grain which might become either bread or wine. And there were earlier gods than Christ associated with the same kind of sacramental feasting. Attis and Adonis are among the instances given by Fraser in *The Golden*

[1] Was this Polonaise a subtle flattery for the Polish king?

Bough. Fraser even tells us that the worship of Adonis, spirit of the corn, was native to Bethlehem, a place-name meaning 'the house of bread.'[1]

Allusion has already been made to the fact that from motives of policy the Christian Church wherever possible took over local beliefs, transmuting them for its own, generally nobler, purposes. But the church was itself variable in its reading of the significance of the sacramental feast. Was it to be a real and practical sharing of food and drink in the communal interest? Was it to be a symbolic meal indicating that those present held common and equalitarian beliefs? Was it to be a communion of a more mystical nature, associating the communism of the feasters with the worship of the vital powers in bread and wine? Was it to be a memorial service associating the natural powers of life with a symbolic perfection of manhood, or godhood? Or was it to be a miraculous changing of natural elements into divine flesh and blood?

All these varying conceptions seem to have been held by different sections of the Christian Church at one time or another;[2] and it is significant that from the most primitive to the most superstitious conception of the Love-Feast a complete cycle of thought was made. Whatever of relation to reality the Church Service pos-

[1] *Adonis, Attis, Osiris*, by J. G. Fraser, Third Edition, pp. 214-5.
[2] *The Philosophy of Civilisation*, by R. H. Towner, II, 48-50; *Handbook of the Early Christian Fathers*, by Leigh-Bennett; Percy Gardner, *The Growth of Christianity*.

sessed seems clearly to have been based on the simple fact that bread and wine could be converted into human strength, and should in a 'holy' or sane community of people be shared in common.

So, when Bach passed beyond the meanness of his Protestant Church, it was not to yield himself to the superstitions of the Roman Church—it was to give the finest expression he could to human ideas which rooted far back in primitive human nature. The B minor Mass is of no ceremonial use to any church. It is just the finest architectural expression of Bach's genius; and all its moods are human from the first *Kyrie* which is not a prayer but a demand, to the *Dona Nobis Pacem* which clearly enough expresses the idea that peace can only be won by those who are prepared to insist upon it. There is no passive pacifism in the music of Bach.

Less personal in superficial conception, less remote in essential meaning are the wonderful chorale-cantatas. Throughout his career the master had used the songs of the people with an increasing sense of their importance. During his last years he devoted himself to them even more emphatically. If he could not serve the cause of the people in any real way, he would at least give his ripest powers to the glorification of their songs, and to the lost cause whence those songs had sprung.

The extraordinary elaboration of Bach's musical style may lead us to forget that it was originally a popular style. That common share which the people had in the greatest works of Gothic architecture had indeed been lost in the greatest of all Gothic music. The artisans who could carve figure-sculpture with Phidia's own skill were in Bach's time no more; there were apparently a few instrumental players of similar skill, but that they were rapidly dying out is shown by the sort of music which was written by the best composers after Bach's death. Nevertheless it was from that old and popular Gothic tradition that Bach's power was obtained, and when he used it to glorify the people's chorales he was but setting jewels in their natural surroundings.

Moreover, complicated though his style has seemed to many later musicians, he was very close to the folk-spirit. His Phoebus and Pan, the Coffee and Peasant Cantatas, and even such movements as *Et Resurrexit*, and the *Et in spiritum sanctum* from the B minor Mass (which I have known to be taken for a Somerset folk-song by a woman living in Somerset), prove the common stuff in which the greatest of all musical geniuses worked.

The method pursued by him in the chorale-cantatas was varied and apparently inexhaustible. In his earlier years at Leipsig he had already written such works— the Easter Cantata, *Christ lag in Todesbanden*, and *Ein feste Burg*—two of Martin Luther's own hymns, with their verses set for solo, duet, trio and chorus, in the form of free and elaborate variations—variations by the side of which Haydn's and Mozart's, and even Beethoven's works in that form, are but elementary play.

A freer course is pursued in the later chorale-cantatas. In some of them two or three tunes are used; but the most satisfactory as art-works are those in which a single tune is treated in two or three important numbers of the work, with intervening and independent numbers by way of episode. Such are *Wachet auf, Das neugeborne, Ach Gott! wie nanches Herzeleid*, belonging to his earlier works in this form; and, among the later and rather simpler works, *Ach Gott von Himmel, Mache dich mein Geist bereit*, and *Schmücke dich o liebe Seele*.

In some of these the tune is blazed out, in others half-hidden; in some the intervening solos are entirely independent, in others they have obvious thematic affinity with the central tune. As indicated on an earlier page, there was no sort of progressive development in the work of Bach when once he had won his polyphonic technic. The latest of these cantatas is the peer and not the progeny of the earlier works in the same form. The only difference between the earliest and the latest is in the direct fighting intention of the former and the secreted significance of the latter. Bach had by this time come to terms with life. He struggled no longer, but retired into a kind of mental isolation and expressed

with increasing austerity and remoteness the faith that
was in him. It was the old popular faith which was
known to him as Pietist. He renounced nothing of his
innermost principles, but just accepted the external
limitations which little minds placed upon his work;
and within those limitations continued to prove his essential power.

What the chorale-cantatas say with some degree of
open expression the chorale-preludes for organ say
with exquisite subterfuge. Here was a form in which
Bach could state every idea in which he believed, and
he did so with such clever obscurity that only during
our own generation have his intentions been realized. A
general willingness to acknowledge the beauty and truth
that expressed a popular cause has always been post-
poned until the cause has been lost. The creative impulse of the common people of Christendom could
scarcely be denied while they were taking their obvious
share in the building of the cathedrals; for those were
days when the popular power was great and growing.
When their international instrument of the Catholic
Church had been weakened by the progressive, financial,
and reactionary feudal classes, and the popular movement was damped down, cathedral building slacked off,
the paintings of the artizans were blotted out with
whitewash, their carols and plays censored, and the
very ritual of the popular tradition given an orthodox

gloss; then all that remained of expression to the Christian spirit were the concealed and sometimes subconscious ideas in the music of Bach—and even that was so far as possible, declared to be a curious scientific exercise, and (especially in the chorale preludes) removed from the intelligible canon of European art. Now that Christianity is dead the feudal and financial coalition can afford to take pride in the cathedrals as museums, to uncover the wall-paintings, take a cultured interest in the mystery-plays, and admit the virtue of the music.

Bach lived to realize that the Heavenly King of Christian faith had been conquered by the money-kings of the earth; but the composer had the satisfaction of receiving a sort of homage from the greatest earthly king of his own time. The music which he wrote for —and in which in some sort he collaborated with— Frederick the Great has little expressional value; but it enabled the old master to assert his personal peerage and keep the parasitic burgher rabble at bay.

Bach lived to realize the final extinction of the medieval hope that the sons of men were also Sons of God—that the Kingdom of Heaven would come on earth; but he was finally true to his cause. Suffering many defeats, and with many vacillations, he held to the last his faith in the essential value of common human beings, and in the greater worth of their creative genius. So with dead eyes and feebling breath he dictated his last tribute to that genius—the chorale-prelude, *Wenn wir in hochsten Nothen sein.*

He died on July 28, 1750, while the Christian nations were preparing for the Seven Years' War, and his own Saxony was selling her sons to Holland and England for the furtherance of their colonial invasions.

✎ Appendix ✎

1. For a fair study of Bach's organ works the edition most useful to English students seems to be that of Messrs. Novello. It is the only edition known to me which includes a volume giving the chorales upon which Bach based so much of his chief organ music; but when so happy an idea occurred to the editor it was a pity that he restricted its value by giving generally only one verse of the words. For full English translations recourse must be made to Professor Terry's three volumes dealing with the chorales, published by the Cambridge University Press.

2. The Easter Cantata does not appear to be yet issued with an English translation. Fortunately, to supply this all too frequent deficiency, Professor Terry has published a volume, Bach Cantata Texts, with English versions of all the sacred and secular cantatas; they are adapted to serve a practical purpose, inasmuch as each sentence is translated with the form of its musical phrase in view.

Three of Kuhnau's Bible Sonatas are published by Messrs. Novello, while the Caprice on the Departure of a Brother can, of course, be obtained in several good editions.

3. Of Bach's earlier organ works there are a few useful records. The Columbia Graphaphone Company issues the following:

Catalogue number.	Work.	Performer and Organ.
9133	Toccata in C major	W. G. Webber, Christ Church, Westminster
9133	Fantasia in C minor	W. G. Webber, Christ Church, Westminster
9552	Fantasia in G minor	E. Commette, Lyons Cathedral
9136	Toccata in D minor	G. T. Pattman, Liberal Jewish Synagogue
9229	Fugue in G major (a la Gigue)	H. Walton, Glasgow Cathedral

The Gramophone Company issues:

D1356	Fantasia and Fugue in C minor.	M. Dupré, Queen's Hall
D1402	Prelude and Fugue in G major.	M. Dupré, Queen's Hall
C1291	Toccata in D minor	G. D. Cunningham, Kingsway Hall
C1452	First movement from Sonata in E flat	W. G. Alcock, Salisbury Cathedral
C1452	Prelude in D major	W. G. Alcock, Salisbury Cathedral
B2654	Fugue in D major	W. G. Alcock, Salisbury Cathedral
C1534-5	Prelude and Fugue in B minor	E. C. Bairstow, York Minster
E424	Prelude and Fugue in G minor (small)	R. Goss-Custard, Kingsway Hall
E416	Fugue in G minor (a la Gigue)	R. Goss-Custard, Kingsway Hall

Of the above records the best are those by M. Dupré. Only he maintains a clear rhythm throughout. The others betray in greater or less degree the besetting sins of organists, in allowing rapid finger-work to run away with the rhythm, and in hanging up the music for changes of registration. The records are none the less of value to students,

were it only in proving to them the evils into which Bach
may be so easily betrayed at the hands of organists. It is
an undoubted fact that first-rate musicians in our time very
seldom take up a career in which the organ is an instrument
of major importance; while the modern organ is itself an
increasingly decadent thing.

Such evils give additional support to the plea upon another
page that the best organ works of Bach should be scored
for orchestra. Schweitzer disapproves of that as contrary
to the spirit of Bach; but the student has only to study
Elgar's orchestral version of the C minor Fantasia and
Fugue (HMV, D1560) or the orchestral version of the Toccata in D minor as played by the Philadelphia Orchestra
under Stowkowski (HMV, D1428), and compare them with
any of the above renderings except those of Dupré, to
understand the difference between the normal organ performance, at the hands and feet of even reputable musicians, and what is possible from the orchestra.

Poor instrument as the piano is, even it can sometimes
give more intense life than the organ, as witness the record
of Mark Hambourg in the Toccata in D minor (HMV,
C1704). A comparison of the last-named work in the four
above-mentioned records should be of real help to the
student of Bach, and to those who seek the best means
of propagating some of the noblest music ever written.

It should be noted that of the works enumerated above
one or two were probably written or revised in Bach's
later years. The majority, however, belong to his time at
Weimar.

4. Throughout Bach's career he seems to have been engaged upon organ arrangements of chorale-tunes. During his

later years at Weimar he made the collection known as the *Orgelbuchlein* (Novello, XV), short examples of the chorale-prelude. I cannot discover that any of these lovely little pieces has been recorded for the gramophone; but one of them, *Ich ruf zu dir*, has been recorded in an orchestral version by the Philadelphia Symphony Orchestra (HMV, D1464).

5. Of the beautiful instrumental works composed during the Cöthen period few have been yet recorded for gramophone; but a useful beginning has been made, especially by The Gramophone Company. First in importance are the Brandenburg Concerto in F major (D1708-10), and the B minor Suite for flute and strings (D1673-4), both played by American Orchestras. Then there is the double violin concerto recorded for the same company by Kreisler, Zimbalist and a string quartet (DB597-8); and for the Columbia Company by Anton and Alma Witek and a string orchestra (9681-2). Personally I prefer the latter recording, which has the advantage of a band, the better to give Bach's conception of the concerto-idea. In the former Kreisler seems outclassed by Zimbalist in the matter of expression. Neither interpretation gives the rapturous peace of what is perhaps the loveliest slow movement ever penned, or the lusty vitality of the allegros. For Columbia Miss Harriet Cohen has played the first eight Preludes and Fugues of the Fortyeight (L2239-2244), and the Gramophone Company issue Herold Samuel's interpretation of the Second English Suite (C1405-6). From the Trio-Sonatas for clavicembalo only one movement has been recorded—upon the organ, by W. G. Alcock (C1452); the pedal part comes through very poorly.

6. The St. Matthew Passion has apparently not yet been recorded as a whole, and only the following arias seem to be available:

No. 47, *Erbarme dich* (Have mercy, God), sung in German by Rosette Anday (HMV, D1664); and No. 58, *Aus Liebe will mein Heiland sterben* (For love my Saviour now is dying), sung by Elizabeth Schumann (HMV, D1410). The latter is in every way nearer the spirit of Bach. The first is a flagrant example of the failure to give full value to Bach's slower movements; and moreover two ugly cuts are made, those responsible apparently not realising that the essence of Bach's later thought is more likely to be contained in the instrumental than in the vocal line. Both performances present a false relation between the singer and the solo instrumentalist. In the first there is a violin and in the second a flute, both obbligati; but both players treat their parts as accompaniment rather than as a part of a duet, and when they reach the final important instrumental section, play it hurriedly as if the real piece had ended when the singer stopped.

That last fault is not to be found in the Aria from Cantata No. 159, which is given on the reverse of the second disc. In this Elizabeth Schumann and Leon Goosens (on the oboe) give a better impression of duet; though a full measure of equality is prevented, I imagine, by reason of the position of the oboe at the recording. The voice is too much on top of us, the instrument much too remote. However, the student can learn, by a comparison of the three numbers, the difference between duets for singers and instrumentalists given (1) with equal disregard for the expressive value of Bach's slow movements, (2) with a less hurried tempo, but not enough realisation on the part of the instrumental soloist that he has the last and most important impression to leave behind; and (3) with most exquisite artistry in both parts, though the instrument fails of its full effect by reason of its relation to the audience. However, the final cadential phrase gives a perfect impression of what a concluding passage ought to be, even in a vocal number.

Unfortunately in the Schumann-Goosens' record the continuo has been played upon a piano, which unpleasantly protrudes its modern self. Compare that with the harpsichord continuo in the Aria from a Christmas Cantata (No. 151) sung by Dora Labette with flue obbligato by Robert Murchie (Columbia 9247), and here, in spite of slight defects in the recording, we have an even better ensemble.

The lovely funeral motet, *Jesu meine Freunde,* may be studied in four records issued by the Gramophone Company (E458-9 and D1256-7), a performance by the London Bach Cantata Club conducted by Kennedy Scott; the English Suite in A minor (C1405-6) played by Harold Samuel—on a modern piano, alas!

7. For a study of the B minor Mass there is at the disposal of the student a fine series of records, issued by the Gramophone Company, giving the complete work. Allowing for the fact that no such records can yet give a present sense of performance, the orchestra and especially the chorus sounding too far off, sometimes even as beyond closed doors, the fact remains that in such records as these a new and invaluable adjunct to musical education is accessible, even for those who have no metropolitan advantages.

Another very important record is the Italian Concerto played on the harpsichord by Mrs. Gordon Woodhouse (HMV, D1281-2). For those whose private study of keyboard music is limited to the modern piano or organ, a record like this opens up a new and much truer idea of Bach's clavier works. Even such a performance as that of the

Courante from the Cello Sonata in C, played with perfect artistry by Senor Segovia upon the guitar (HMV, E475), is nearer to the spirit of Bach than any ordinary piano performance can be.

Of the later organ works a few are available for the gramophone. The Fantasia in G minor, played by M. Commette upon the organ of Lyons Cathedral (Columbia, 9552); the Prelude and Fugue in B minor, played by Dr Bairstow upon the organ of York Minister (HMV, 1534-5), and the following organ-chorales: *Christ unser Herr zum Jordan kam*, played by M. Dupré upon Queen's Hall Organ (HMV, E471), or by Dr A. W. Wilson on the organ of Manchester Cathedral (Columbia, 9501); *Nun komm der Heiden Heiland*, played by Dr Bairstow in York Minster; *Wachet auf*, played by M. Dupré (HMV, E471); and two chorales played by Dr Albert Schweitzer upon the organ at Queen's Hall (HMV, C1543), one being *Wenn wir in hochsten Nothen sind*, the last work of Bach's life.

The best organ records are those of Dupré and Schweitzer, though even they are not without serious defects—the first in the undue swamping of the figural work by the tune, and the second in that a too restrained effect is given, as though the performer sought to revive the effects of Bach's own organ rather than the reality of his music.

None of the church-cantatas seem to have been recorded. Considering the importance of the cantatas and the chorale-preludes in the study of the master's work, it is to be hoped that they will receive special attention in the near future, for the growing body of Bach students is undeniable.

One other record deserves special attention—the orchestrated performance of the chorale *Wir glauben all an einen Gott*, sometimes called the Giant Fugue. This is recorded in a performance by the Philadelphia Orchestra (HMV, D1710); and in my view entirely disposes of any objections which may be entertained regarding the justice of the proceeding. It brings out every separate part, which even so fine an artist as M. Dupré could not do; it gives a variety of colour which is deliberately absent from the performances of Dr Schweitzer, but is justified, I think, when we recall the love Bach had for all the colour effects that were available to him; and finally, in the degradation of the modern organ owing to the influence of the cinema-trusts on the one hand, and the acoustics of many churches on the other (for example York Minster, which causes Dr Bairstow to fail of clearness in both rhythm and phrase), what was Bach's own chief medium of expression is no longer open to us, even if we had not outgrown it. The orchestra is the only fitting medium for this greatest of all music, and its transference has the authority of the noblest of living composers. Elgar's orchestral version of the *Fantasia and Fugue in C minor* is superb (HMV, D1560).

The ancient harpsichord and the modern orchestra are more essentially musical and expressive than the modern piano and the ancient organ; therefore they are the more suited to the works of the composer who was not only the greatest musical craftsman who ever lived, but was also the deepest and subtlest interpreter of human feeling.

INDEX

"Ach Gott von Himmel," 270
"Ach Gott! wie manches Herze-
    leid," 270
"Actus Tragicus," significance of,
    162 *et seq.*
Adonis, Attis, Osiris, J. G. Fraser,
    267
Aeschylus, Bach compared to, 228
Agamemnon, Murray's transla-
    tion, 228
Alexander VI, pope, 104
Angelico, Fra, 2
Annunzio, Gabriele d', 173
Appreciation, caused by dissatis-
    faction, 12
    evaluation of our, 6 *et seq.*
    inconstancy of wealthy in, 8
        et seq.
    of Bach as an orthodox musi-
        cian, 15
Architecture, cathedral building,
    20 *et seq.*
    Gothic tradition, 137 *et seq.,*
        269
    parallel in music, 128 *et seq.,*
        132 *et seq.,* 148
    Renaissance, 138
Arnstadt, Bach's activities at, 70
    et seq.
Art, Bach's definition, 243
    climax in, 240 *et seq.*
    clues to the real nature of
        Bach's, 15
    decadent at Weimar, 129
    euphony in, 150
    formality of Bach's, 3 *et seq.*
    great communal, 45, 186 *et
        seq.*

Art—(*Continued*)
    inevitability of Bach's, 23
    in Middle Ages, 20 *et seq.*
    inspiration in, 244
    novelties in, 135 *et seq.*
    pre-war definition, 10
    product of environment, 2 *et
        seq.,* 211 *et seq.*
    religious tendencies in, 9
    soul of creative, 2
    superficial characteristics of
        Renaissance, 23
    without emotion impossible, 12
Atkins, Sir Ivor, 256

Bach, Anna Magdalena, debt
    owed, 265
Bach, Hans, 73
Bach, John Sebastian, ancestors,
    37, 123 *et seq.*
    and Christian struggle insep-
        arable, 52, 56 *et seq.,* 73
    and the Italian style, 130 *et
        seq.,* 144, 174
    as Cantor, 3
    as organist, 67
    at St. Michael's Convent, 37 *et
        seq.*
    birth, 36
    character, 74, 78 *et seq.,* 92,
        120, 158, 265
    choice of subject, 85
    Concert-master at Weimar, 154
    devices used by, 65, 82 *et seq.,*
        146 *et seq.*
    executive artist, 126 *et seq.*
    factual quality of, 64
    figurative imagination, 65

INDEX

INDEX

Dante, 2, 80
  exile, 25
"Das neugeborne," 270
Debussy, Claude, debt owed, 204
Dent, Professor, on Mozart's operas, 184
"Die Elenden sollen essen," 233
Divine Comedy, Dante, 58
"D Major Fugue," use of chords, 149
"D Major Prelude," use of chords, 149
Dowland, John, 120
Drama, as used by Bach, 168 *et seq.*
  evolution in, 217 *et seq.*
Duets, for treble and alto, 241
Dürer, Albrecht, 62
"Du wahrer Gott und David's Sohn," discussion of, 230 *et seq.*
  translation of, 191

"Easter Cantata," interpretation, 74 *et seq.*
Eight Chapters on Medieval Art, Prior, 21, 52
Eilmar, friend of Bach, 121
"Ein feste Burg," based on Luther's hymns, 269
  occasion for writing, 258
Elgar, Sir Edward, 11
  criticism of, 256
  orchestral version, 276
English House, The, Shaw Sparrow, 44
Ernst, Duke Johann, Bach in household of, 68

Feast of Rose-Garlands, The, Dürer, 63, *note*
Fitzwillian Virginals Book, 196
  use of keynote in, 201 *et seq.*
Folk songs, Bach's use of, 115
  importance of, 127 *et seq.*
  in England, 128
  in Russia, 128

Folk songs—(*Continued*)
  Italian, 173
  tradition in Germany, 128
  use in religion, 113
  vindication by Bach, 259 *et seq.*
  (*see also* Chorales)
Forkel, Johann, on Bach, xi
"Forty-Eight Preludes and Fugues," variety of keys used, 195, 204 *et seq.*
Frederick the Great, king, music for, 272
"French Suite in B Minor," modulations in, 203
"French Suites," written for son, 195 *et seq.*
Fugue, structure, 141 *et seq.*
  various stages in Bach's, 147
"Fugue in G Major," evaluated, 131

Galileo, 138
Gay, John, 36
Germany, after the Lutheran compromise, 45 *et seq.*
  contrapuntal style in, 66
  mass-expression in, 246
  of Bach, 30 *et seq.*
  popular religious songs of, 43
Germany, A. W. Holland, 105
Gesner, aids Bach, 260
Gesualdo, Don Carlo, Bach's predecessor, 7
Gevaert, on musical piracy, 39
Giotto, 23, 140
Goethe, Johann, 14
Golden Bough, The, Fraser, 218, 266
"Gottes Zeit," duet in, 176
  evaluation of, 161 *et seq.*
Gounod, Charles, 8
Goya, Francisco, 2
Gregory X, pope, 24
  reaction to hymns, 40 *et seq.*
Growth of Christianity, The, Percy Gardner, 267

~286~

INDEX